EYE ON ART

Michelangelo
Master of the Renaissance

By Tamra B. Orr

Portions of this book originally appeared in *Michelangelo* by Phyllis Raybin Emert.

Published in 2019 by
Lucent Press, an Imprint of Greenhaven Publishing, LLC
353 3rd Avenue
Suite 255
New York, NY 10010

Designer: Deanna Paternostro
Editor: Melissa Raé Shofner

Library of Congress Cataloging-in-Publication Data

Names: Orr, Tamra, author.
Title: Michelangelo : master of the Renaissance / Tamra B. Orr.
Description: New York : Lucent Press, 2019. | Series: Eye on art | Includes
   bibliographical references and index.
Identifiers: LCCN 2018023714 (print) | LCCN 2018025753 (ebook) | ISBN
   9781534565357 (eBook) | ISBN 9781534565340 (library bound book) | ISBN
   9781534565371 (pbk. book)
Subjects: LCSH: Michelangelo Buonarroti, 1475-1564–Juvenile literature. |
   Artists–Italy–Biography–Juvenile literature. | Art,
   Renaissance–Italy–Juvenile literature.
Classification: LCC N6923.B9 (ebook) | LCC N6923.B9 O77 2019 (print) | DDC
   709.2 [B] –dc23
LC record available at https://lccn.loc.gov/2018023714

Printed in the United States of America

CPSIA compliance information: Batch #BW19KL. For further information contact Greenhaven Publishing LLC, New York, New York at 1-844-317-7404.

Please visit our website, www.greenhavenpublishing.com. For a free color catalog of all our high-quality books, call toll free 1-844-317-7404 or fax 1-844-317-7405.

Contents

Foreword

What is art? There is no one answer to that question. Every person has a different idea of what makes something a work of art. Some people think of art as the work of masters such as Leonardo da Vinci, Mary Cassatt, or Michelangelo. Others see artistic beauty in everything from skyscrapers and animated films to fashion shows and graffiti. Everyone brings their own point of view to their interpretation of art.

Discovering the hard work and pure talent behind artistic techniques from different periods in history and different places around the world helps people develop an appreciation for art in all its varied forms. The stories behind great works of art and the artists who created them have fascinated people for many years and continue to do so today. Whether a person has a passion for painting, graphic design, or another creative pursuit, learning about the lives of great artists and the paths that can be taken to achieve success as an artist in the modern world can inspire budding creators to pursue their dreams.

This series introduces readers to different artistic styles, as well as the artists who made those styles famous. As they read about creative expression in the past and present, they are challenged to think critically about their own definition of art.

Quotes from artists, art historians, and other experts provide a unique perspective on each topic, and a detailed bibliography is provided as a starting place for further research. In addition, a list of websites and books about each topic encourages readers to continue their exploration of the fascinating world of art.

This world comes alive with each turn of the page, as readers explore sidebars about the artistic process and creative careers. Essential examples of different artistic styles are presented in the form of vibrant photographs and historical images, giving readers a comprehensive look at art history from ancient times to the present.

Art may be difficult to define, but it is easy to appreciate. In developing a deeper understanding of different art forms, readers will be able to look at the world around them with a fresh perspective on the beauty that can be found in unexpected places.

An Artistic Genius

Michelangelo di Lodovico Buonarroti Simoni—commonly known by just his first name, Michelangelo—was one of the greatest artists of all time. He gave the world some of the most magnificent artwork ever created. The world knows far more about him than about many other artists of his time for several reasons. First, he lived much longer than the average person during the Renaissance. The average life span during this time was between 35 and 40 years, and Michelangelo lived half a century more than that. He continued working into his 70s and 80s, which gave both historians and average people plenty of paintings and sculptures to admire and study. Second, Michelangelo wrote many letters. Out of the more than 1,400 letters sent to and from him, almost 500 have been published in English. Each one provides great insight into who this man truly was and what he thought about. Finally, the artist collaborated on projects with hundreds of people, and those interactions often appear in other records.

Recognized as an artistic genius in his own time, Michelangelo focused on the beauty, movement, and expression of the human body. During his lifetime, which was from 1475 to 1564, both religious and secular society had a high regard for the classical art of ancient Greece and Rome, and this greatly influenced Michelangelo's work during the Italian Renaissance after the Middle Ages.

In the second half of his life, Michelangelo began to embrace Mannerism, an art form that was a reaction to the classical forms of beauty. Whereas the art of the Renaissance embraced grace, harmony, and lifelike subjects, Mannerism focused on unrealistic and exaggerated poses and elongated and twisted limbs. Many of Michelangelo's later major works tended toward Mannerism with a distortion of scale and perspective and agitated body movements of the subjects.

During Michelangelo's final years, people's attitudes toward art changed dramatically. The Protestant Reformation was in action, attempting to correct the abuses of the Roman Catholic Church. Protestant churches rose in power, and the Catholic churches fought back with the Counter-Reformation. Suddenly, the use of nudity in art was prohibited. Artwork was to only illustrate Biblical scenes. A painting or sculpture was judged on its religious instructional value, not on artistic achievement or beauty. Artwork of the naked human body was considered indecent, and Michelangelo's works were criticized. It was the end of the Italian Renaissance.

While Michelangelo was still alive, two major biographies were written about him. The first, written by Italian painter and biographer Giorgio Vasari, came out in 1550 and focused on Michelangelo as an artist. The second was published three years later by Michelangelo's student Ascanio Condivi. Condivi's biography contains material from Michelangelo himself that had not been included in Vasari's work. Vasari then published a revised and expanded second edition in 1568, which includes details from Condivi and information about the years leading up to the artist's death in 1564.

Over the years, Michelangelo has earned some of the highest praise, being called everything from the "greatest artist of all time"[1] and the "genius of the Renaissance"[2] to the first "superstar artist."[3] Vasari believed that Michelangelo was a gift from God. He wrote, "The great Ruler of Heaven looked down and ... resolved ... to send to earth a genius universal in each art, to show single-handed the perfection of line and shadow." According to Vasari, "He was sent into the world by God to help artists to learn from his life, his character, and his works what a true artist should be."[4]

Michelangelo was a man of many contradictions. He was described as tightfisted and quick tempered, yet generous with his family and friends. Vasari stated, "Although rich he lived like a poor man."[5] Michelangelo financially supported some of his bothersome dependent relatives, yet he loved them and worked hard all his life to reestablish and elevate the family name of Buonarroti.

According to biographers, despite his success, Michelangelo was not a happy man. Art conservator and Michelangelo

Renaissance paintings, such as this one by Caravaggio, were often meant to teach and reinforce religious lessons.

expert Antonio Forcellino wrote in his book *Michelangelo: A Tormented Life* that "[Michelangelo] trusted no one ... He always feared deceit, persecution and fraud. He lived like a wretch." Forcellino also referred to the "miseries, conflicts, and sufferings" of Michelangelo's life, which was "ordinary in its grimness."[6]

Michelangelo managed to survive the changing times he lived in, outliving both his competitive rivals and controlling popes—rulers of the Catholic Church. He lived to age 88, a rarity in the 16th century. His artistic gifts, even in his early years, were recognized by many, including rulers, patrons of the arts, and popes. These relationships enabled him to create works of beauty such as the *David*, the *Pietà*, the Sistine Chapel ceiling, *The Last Judgment*, and the architecture of St. Peter's Basilica. Even Michelangelo's poetry was beautiful. He wrote sonnets to his friends, family, and acquaintances about the enduring topics of art and beauty, faith, love, and death.

In his biography of Michelangelo, Vasari wrote that when Michelangelo was asked by a friend why he never married and had children, the artist replied that his wives were his art and his works were his children, "and they will live a while however valueless."[7] Michelangelo was right, as his works will live forever as priceless masterpieces to admire and inspire.

CHAPTER ONE

A Family, a Struggle, and a Choice

The Buonarroti Simoni family was struggling. For years, the family line had been well respected in Italy. Their ancestors had lived in Florence for generations. However, by the time Lodovico di Leonardo Buonarroti Simoni married Francesca di Neri del Miniato del Sera in 1472, the family had fallen on financial hard times. When he was offered a six-month position as *podestà*, or mayor, of the Italian mountain villages of Caprese and Chiusi, it was a welcome relief. He and Francesa already had one son, and their second was due soon. The family was given a stone house to live in and a salary that paid for several clerks, servants, and a horseman.

Michelangelo was born on March 6, 1475, in Caprese in the early morning hours. The name Michelangelo—after the archangel Michael, who Catholics believed brought souls to judgment, rescued the faithful, and fought against evil—was an unusual choice for the time. Chiusi had a church dedicated to the archangel, and some historians suspect Michelangelo's father named his second son in honor of the village and church.

Chisel and Hammer

When Michelangelo was only a month old, his father's position as *podestà* ended. The Buonarrotis returned to the small family farm inherited

Michelangelo's family was given a stone house to live in while in Caprese. The house is shown here.

from Michelangelo's grandfather in Settignano, Italy. They immediately put their young infant in the care of a local wet nurse, a woman hired to nurse and care for the child. Wealthy, upper-class families often did this, and the child was returned to the household once they reached the age of about two or three.

The wet nurse was the daughter and wife to stonecutters. As an adult, Michelangelo joked that being a sculptor was passed down to him through his wet nurse, and that is why he loved working with stone. He told Vasari that "along with the milk of my nurse I received the knack of handling chisel and hammer, with which I make my figures."[8]

A Family of Sons

Michelangelo and his older brother, Lionardo, were soon joined by three additional brothers.

Although historians are not sure of the source of Michelangelo's name, some suspect he was named after the archangel Michael (shown here).

"Down Like Biscuit"

Michelangelo was so confident about his abilities as an artist that some might have described him as arrogant. Pietro Torrigiani was an artist who frequently painted in the same garden as Michelangelo and one day, the two of them came to blows:

Michelangelo never thought he was an attractive man, in part because of injuring his nose as a youth.

Buonarroti and I used, when we were boys, to go into the Church of the Carmine to learn drawing from the Chapel of Masaccio. It was Buonarroti's habit to banter all who were drawing there, and one day, when he was annoying me, I got more angry than usual, and, clenching my fist, gave him such a blow on the nose that I felt bone and cartilage go down like biscuit beneath my knuckles; and this mark of mine he will carry with him to the grave.[1]

Michelangelo biographer Ascanio Condivi wrote about the same incident in *The Life of Michelangelo*: "When he was a boy, a man called Torrigiano [Pietro] de' Torrigiani, a brutal and arrogant person; with a blow of his fist almost broke the cartilage of Michelangelo's nose, so that he was carried home as if dead. However, that Torrigiani who was banished from Florence for this, came to a bad end."[2]

Whether Torrigiani really was banished from Florence is not known, but he did leave for Rome, Italy, sometime after this incident. Michelangelo's nose never healed properly, and his face was forever marked by his conspicuously flat and somewhat crooked nose.

1. Quoted in John T. Spike, *Young Michelangelo: The Path to the Sistine*. New York, NY: Vendome Press, 2010.
2. Quoted in Spike, *Young Michelangelo*.

Buonarroto was born in 1477, Giovansimone followed two years later, and then Gismondo two years after that. After Gismondo's birth, young Francesca died, leaving five sons, between the ages of infancy and eight. Four years later, Michelangelo's father married Lucrezia di Antonio Ubaldini da Gagliano.

Author and journalist George Bull described Michelangelo as an "alert, sensitive, intelligent, introspective and quick-tempered boy, prone to sickness, but resilient, with black hair and brown eyes flecked with yellow."[9] Some art historians believe the lack of a relationship with his mother or maternal affection made Michelangelo afraid of women. Others disagree. William E. Wallace wrote in *Michelangelo: The Artist, The Man, and His Times*, that "Michelangelo displays a profound sensitivity to feminine beauty and a special tenderness for Christ's mother, who is one of the most frequent figures in his art. Themes of maternal love, loss, and separation abound in Michelangelo's art and poetry."[10]

Michelangelo was not close to his father, either. He was embarrassed by his father's inability to keep a job and by the family's financial strains. Although Michelangelo's father sent him to receive formal schooling, Michelangelo's main interest was in drawing and painting, not academics. He used every spare moment to draw pictures of everything he saw, from local buildings and churches to sculptures and paintings.

Making a Friend

Michelangelo's life changed dramatically when he met an older boy named Francesco Granacci. Granacci was an apprentice in the art studio of Domenico and Davide Ghirlandaio, who were two well-known painters in Florence. Granacci managed to get 13-year-old Michelangelo taken in as another apprentice. It was a true turning point in the young artist's life—but it did not come without a high price.

Michelangelo's father was not happy about his son's new passion for art. He did not believe it was an acceptable occupation for a gentleman; painters were people who only worked with their hands. Condivi wrote, "[Michelangelo's] father and his uncles, who held the art in contempt, were much displeased, and often beat him severely for it: they were so ignorant of the excellence and nobility of art that they thought shame to have her in the house. This, however much he disliked it, was not enough to turn him back, but, on the contrary, made him more bold."[11]

Eventually his father agreed, and Michelangelo joined Granacci and other young men in learning art and painting. In return, Domenico Ghirlandaio agreed to pay Michelangelo a salary. Writers such as Forcellino believe Michelangelo's father likely agreed to his son's enrollment mainly because the family needed the money. However, he most likely resigned himself to the idea that

Michelangelo created this drawing, which is a study of how fabric folded, in the early 1500s.

Michelangelo would never be part of the upper classes and would instead be stuck in the artisan, working class.

Art Lessons

Michelangelo's days at the workshop were full of important lessons. He, along with the other apprentices, were taught about design and coloring techniques, drawing with pen and brush, and fresco painting from books, live models, and on-the-job experience. According to Forcellino,

> The apprentice had to learn to look after the tools of the trade and keep them in complete working order. Then he had to become familiar with the materials ... Only when an apprentice was completely expert with every material and its use, could he start to work as a genuine assistant to his more senior colleagues: preparing the surfaces for painting, spreading the glue and chalk primer over wooden surfaces ... and painting in small portions of the background.[12]

In his limited spare time, Michelangelo practiced his skills by copying models in the workshop and works of great artists. In many cases, Michelangelo copied so accurately that few could tell the original and the copy apart. The young artist even used smoke to make the paintings look timeworn. Soon, he had surpassed the other students and sometimes even the teachers. Ghirlandaio commented to Giorgio Vasari that Michelangelo knew more than he did.

It is possible that Ghirlandaio was envious of his arrogant but talented young pupil. When he was asked by Florentine ruler Lorenzo de' Medici to send his best students to his San Marco garden to create some sculptures, Ghirlandaio happily recommended teenage Michelangelo and Granacci. Michelangelo's father was even more upset that his son wanted to become a sculptor, which he viewed as nothing but a glorified stonecutter—but Michelangelo's mind was made up.

A Faun's Missing Teeth

The Medici garden of San Marco was an astonishing place of natural beauty, filled with trees, flowers, and Medici's collection of ancient and modern statues, frescoes, paintings, and drawings. The garden was surrounded by high walls, and the property included a house and sleeping quarters. Young, talented artists were invited here to study, copy, and create artwork under the supervision of well-known sculptor Bertoldo di Giovanni.

Among Michelangelo's first projects was the reproduction of the head of a faun in marble. Medici praised the workmanship and technique of the piece, but he joked to the young man that the faun was very old and should be missing some of its teeth. After Medici left, Michelangelo chiseled away a few of the teeth. When the Prince of Florence returned, he was impressed by the seriousness of the young artist and the beauty of the finished work.

His First Works in the Garden

While at the Medici garden, Michelangelo sculpted the *Head of a Faun*, as well as the *Madonna of the Stairs* and the *Battle of the Centaurs*. The *Madonna of the Stairs* is a small stone carving measuring 22 inches by 15.75 inches (55.88 cm by 40 cm). Mary, in profile, is seated in the foreground and takes up the entire space. On her lap is the Christ child with his back to the viewer and his face hidden from sight. Mary gazes off into the distance as she lifts her cloak to shelter the child. There are smaller, shallower figures of children on the steps and a railing behind the dominant figure of Mary.

Michelangelo decided to carve the *Battle of the Centaurs* after he heard the story of the mythological battle. Bull described the work: "The small, highly polished but unfinished relief shows part of a mêlée [brawl] of athletic male nudes linked in close embrace, with set faces and … expressive bodies."[13] In *Battle of the Centaurs* Michelangelo concentrated on the naked human body engaged in vigorous activity, a theme that would become the focus of his future work.

Medici believed Michelangelo was destined for greatness and convinced Michelangelo's father to allow the young artist to live with the Medicis. Michelangelo soon moved in and shared the home with Medici's three sons, four daughters, and nephew, as well as an array of philosophers, poets, and scholars who visited frequently. Medici eventually secured a simple public service job in Florence for Michelangelo's father. According to Condivi, Medici

> gave Michael Angelo a good room in his own house with all that he needed, treating him like a son, with a seat at his table, which was frequented every day by noblemen and men of great affairs … by all of them Michael Angelo was caressed and incited to his honourable work; but above all by the Magnificent, who would often call for him many times in the day to show him engraved gems … medals, and such like things of great price, seeing that he had genius and good judgment.[14]

A Time of Grief

Medici fell ill suddenly and died on April 8, 1492, at the age of 43. While Florence had lost a diplomat and statesman, Michelangelo had lost a friend, a mentor, and a patron. The artist returned to his father's home to grieve. There, he learned that his

Michelangelo sculpted the Madonna of the Stairs *around 1491, when he was only about 17 years old.*

The Medicis and the Arts

The Medicis were prosperous and well-known figures during the Italian Renaissance, largely because of their successful bank with branches throughout Europe. The bank played a significant role in trade and commerce, and the family's accumulated wealth led to political power. Lorenzo de' Medici, like his father and grandfather before him, amassed great wealth, power, and patronage, and he was determined to continue the Medici family dominance. Under his leadership, Florence blossomed as the center of Renaissance art and learning. The city was the home of the Platonic Academy, where scholars discussed philosophy and the classics, religious plays were staged, and festivals were held throughout the area. There were jousting tournaments, dances, fencing competitions, and even a horse race to celebrate the feast day of St. John.

older brother, Lionardo, had become a monk. Michelangelo's family was struggling financially, and his father hoped that Michelangelo would quickly find paid commissions from a new patron. At first, Michelangelo was too sad over the death of Medici, but eventually he decided to learn all he could about human anatomy to help him become a better sculptor.

Understanding the Body

Michelangelo wanted his human figures to appear as realistic and alive as possible, so he chose to study them firsthand by dissecting human corpses. Although the Church was hesitant to allow dissection, the artist's skill and talent convinced the prior of the Church of Santo Spirito to allow Michelangelo appropriate space and subjects for detailed study.

Michelangelo made many anatomical drawings that helped him better understand the muscles, bones, and tissues involved in human movement. In return for the kindness shown to him by the prior of Santo Spirito, in 1493, Michelangelo made him a life-size wooden crucifix for the high altar of the church.

While Michelangelo was learning a great deal, the methods were difficult for him. Condivi wrote that he

gave up dissection because it turned his stomach so that he could neither eat nor drink with benefit ... [but] he did not give up until he was so learned and rich in such knowledge that he often had in his mind the wish to write, for the sake of sculptors and painters, a treatise on the movements of the human body.[15]

It was important to Michelangelo that he capture the muscles and shapes of human bodies accurately in his drawings and sculptures.

After finishing his anatomical studies, Michelangelo bought a large block of marble. Around 1493, he created a statue of the Greek hero Hercules, son of Zeus, known for his immense strength. The statue was about 7 feet 7.5 inches (2.33 m) tall, according to Condivi. It was purchased by the wealthy Strozzi family in Florence. Eventually, the *Hercules* made its way to the court of the king of France, and then historians lost track of it.

Fleeing to Safety

Condivi wrote of a big snowstorm in Florence while Michelangelo was living with his father. Medici's son Piero wanted a statue made of snow in the courtyard, so he asked Michelangelo to create one. Michelangelo agreed and created the statue out of snow and ice in the palazzo courtyard. It did not thaw for a week, so many Florentines got the opportunity to see and admire the piece. Piero was so pleased with it, he asked Michelangelo to move back to the Medici palace, and Michelangelo accepted his invitation.

When Piero was only 20 years old, he assumed the position of his late father. Sadly, he lacked the wisdom, diplomacy, and grace of the late Medici. This lack of leadership, childish ways, and abuse of power made him unpopular. When Charles VII of France marched into Italy in 1494 to claim the city-state of Naples, he attacked Florentine towns along the way. Piero went to negotiate with the French king without informing the city government. He ended up giving in to French demands, allowing them to pass through Florence. The city rose up against him.

Seeing what was happening with his patron family and recognizing the possibility of a revolution, Michelangelo secretly and quietly left Florence. He did not want to be associated with the Medicis anymore.

CHAPTER TWO

Trying His Luck Elsewhere

Michelangelo did not know where to go now that he had left Florence and the Medici family behind. He tried living in Venice, Italy, but no one knew him there. They were not willing to take a risk and commission a piece of artwork from just anyone. He decided to go to Tuscany, Italy, but on the way there, he passed through the city of Bologna, Italy. He, along with his companions, entered the city, not knowing that Bologna required all visitors to get a red wax seal on their thumbnails before entering. Moments later, Michelangelo was caught, taken into custody by local security forces, and fined. Michelangelo had no money whatsoever and was kept in detention until nobleman Gianfrancesco Aldrovandi found out he was there. Knowing Michelangelo's work and history with the Medicis, Aldrovandi ordered that the artist be released. Then, he invited Michelangelo to come and live as a guest at his house. Aldrovandi also offered Michelangelo a small sum to create several statues for the tomb of St. Dominic in the Church of San Domenico. The sculptor made *Angel Bearing a Candlestick* (also known as *Candelabrum Angel*) as well as the figures of *St. Petronius* and *St. Proculus*, with each sculpture measuring between 1 and 2 feet (30 and 60.1 cm) tall.

Angel Bearing a Candlestick *was one of several sculptures Michelangelo created for the Church of San Domenico in the late 1400s.*

In 1495, Michelangelo went home for a few months and carved two new pieces, *Young John the Baptist*, commissioned by Lorenzo di Pierfrancesco (a relative of the Medici family), and the *Sleeping Cupid*.

When a Lie Goes Well

Everyone agrees that Michelangelo's *Sleeping Cupid* statue was based on a lie, but who was to blame is something historians still disagree about. It all started when Michelangelo's friend Pierfrancesco supposedly suggested that the *Sleeping Cupid* would sell for far more money if it looked like an antique that had been buried in the earth for years. Either Michelangelo or an art dealer named Baldassari del Milanese artificially aged the sculpture by burying it in a vineyard. The statue was then sold to Italian cardinal Raffaele Riario.

The cardinal was furious when he discovered that the *Sleeping Cupid* was not an antique. He demanded his money back from del Milanese, but, thanks to people's attitudes about art at the time, he was not angry with Michelangelo. Instead, the cardinal was impressed with the young artist's talent and invited him to come to Rome.

A Life-Size Figure

Cardinal Riario had a personal collection of classical statues, and now he wanted Michelangelo to add to that collection. He bought a large block of marble and commissioned the artist to create a life-size figure. This became the statue of *Bacchus*. The money Michelangelo earned from this statue was the equivalent of what his father would have earned in six years with his customs job.

Condivi described the completed *Bacchus*: "This work in form and bearing in every part corresponds to the description of the ancient writers—his aspect, merry; the eyes, squinting and lascivious, like those of people excessively given to the love of wine. He holds a cup in his right hand, like one about to drink, and looks at it lovingly, taking pleasure in the liquor of which he was the inventor."[16] Giorgio Vasari noted the androgynous nature of the statue, "blending in the limbs of the slenderness of a youth and the fleshy roundness of a woman."[17]

According to art historian John T. Spike, the cardinal was not pleased with the statue; he felt it was inappropriate for a man of the church since it portrayed excessive drunkenness and sexuality. Michelangelo had carved the *Bacchus* at the home of wealthy banker Iacopo Gallo. The cardinal never took delivery of the statue, and presumably Gallo purchased the piece for himself and kept it at his home.

Gallo was impressed by the talented Michelangelo and became his patron. He commissioned the young sculptor to carve a beautiful life-size cupid called *Young Archer* (also known as *Apollo*) of white Carrara marble, holding a bow and arrows. Months later, Gallo recommended Michelangelo to the French cardinal Jean de Bilhères de Lagraulas, who wanted a sculpture to decorate his tomb in St. Peter's Basilica.

Out of White Marble: The *Pietà*

Michelangelo was instructed by the cardinal to travel to Carrara to get a large block of white marble. It measured at least 6 feet by 6 feet by 4 feet (1.83 m by 1.83 m by 1.22 m). The entire journey, including time spent picking out the block, cutting it, and transporting it by cart and then by sea back to Rome, took more than six months.

Spike quoted some of the terms in the original contract, from August 1498:

Maestro Michelangelo, statuary of Florence ... shall at his own proper costs make a Pietà of marble, that is to say a draped figure of the Virgin Mary with the dead Christ in her arms, the figures being life-size, for the sum of four hundred and fifty gold ducats in papal gold, to be finished within the term of one year from the beginning of the work ...

And I, Iacopo Gallo, do promise the Most Reverend Monsignore, that the said Michelangelo shall

Thoughts Through Letters

The writings of Michelangelo provide insight into his opinions on art, beauty, family, love, religion, death, and work at various times of his life. Nearly half of his letters were written to his family, offering advice, criticisms, and complaints on everyday matters. In a letter to his father from August 19, 1497, Michelangelo wrote,

[Buonarroto] tells me that the merchant, Consiglio, is giving you a lot of trouble, that he won't come to any agreement and that he wants to have you arrested. I advise you to come to an agreement and pay him a few ducats on account; and whatever you agree to give him, let me know, and I'll send it to you, if you don't have it. Although I have very little money, as I've told you, I'll contrive to borrow it ... Don't be surprised if sometimes I have written so irritably. Often I get wrought up by the sort of things that happen to people away from home. Whatever you ask of me, I will send you.[1]

1. Quoted in John T. Spike, *Young Michelangelo: The Path to the Sistine.* New York, NY: Vendome Press, 2010, p. 106.

complete said work within one year and that it shall be more beautiful than any work in marble to be seen in Rome today, and such that no master of our own time shall be able to produce a better.[18]

Michelangelo fulfilled the contract in every way but one: It took him almost two years to complete the statue because he spent months carefully polishing the marble. Condivi briefly described the completed *Pietà*: "The Madonna is seated on the stone upon which the Cross was erected, with her dead son on her lap. He is of so great and so rare a beauty, that no one beholds it but is moved to pity."[19]

Praise and Criticism

The *Pietà*, finished in 1499, made 24-year-old Michelangelo famous for his beautiful works of art. He did not get glowing praise from everyone, however. Some critics complained that the Madonna looked too young in comparison to her son.

Professor of art history Joachim Poeschke, however, noted that the positioning of the figures shows the contrast between life, death, grief, and beauty. In his book *Michelangelo and His World: Sculpture of the Italian Renaissance*, Poeschke analyzed the *Pietà*: "The nude Christ is almost completely framed by the outline of the wide, flowing robe of Mary," he wrote. Michelangelo "managed to balance the vertical orientation of the one figure and the horizontal, or diagonal, line of the other by placing Mary's right foot higher than her left and creating long curving folds below the body of her son. Mary is presenting his corpse to the viewer, inviting us to gaze upon him with the gesture of her left hand."[20]

The *Pietà* is the only sculpture by Michelangelo that he signed. Vasari related a story that visitors gazing at the *Pietà* credited another artist as the sculptor. This supposedly angered Michelangelo so much that he carved his name on the sash across Mary's

The Pietà is framed beautifully as it sits in Saint Peter's Basilica in Vatican City.

chest. William E. Wallace wrote, "The Pieta is a miracle of marble carving: Michelangelo transformed hard rock into soft flesh and drapery, creating a … two-figure sculpture group of great dignity and breathtaking beauty."[21]

Heading Home

When Michelangelo wrote to his father, he pleaded poverty when asked for money. The artist lived very simply, paying little for his lodgings and rarely sleeping or eating. However, according to Spike, by 1500, Michelangelo's bank account "already contained more money than his father earned in ten years."[22]

In 1501, Michelangelo accepted a commission from Cardinal Francesco Todeschini Piccolomini, who later became Pope Pius III, to carve 15 small figures for the family altar in the cathedral at Siena, Italy. Since he was required to get measurements at Siena and then obtain marble at Carrara, Michelangelo decided to return to Florence after five years and work on the figures at home. He never finished this commission as he became distracted by other projects. In the end, Michelangelo completed only four of the fifteen statues: *St. Peter, St. Paul, St. Gregory,* and *St. Augustine.*

Creating the Giant

When Michelangelo returned to Florence, he was welcomed back with open arms. He kept busy with both private commissions and a very large public one. A huge block of marble had been purchased 35 years earlier for a statue of the biblical king David for the Cathedral of Florence. Several sculptors had begun carving the stone but abandoned their projects, and the block was put aside in the courtyard, neglected and forgotten. Michelangelo signed a contract with the Guild of Wool Merchants, who maintained the cathedral, to carve the "giant," as the *David* was called. He worked on it from 1501 to 1504.

Umberto Baldini, former director of artwork conservation at the Uffizi Gallery in Florence, called the *David* the turning point in Michelangelo's career. "All the positive values that he had gathered in observing the antique and practicing it," Baldini wrote, "all his exercises and direct studies on the human body, all the internal spiritual forces that he had thrown into interpreting the world both in myth and reality: all come into play [in the *David*]."[23]

According to Wallace, a laser scanner measured the *David* at nearly 17 feet (5.18 m) tall. During his work, Michelangelo had a wooden shed put up to shield himself and the marble block from public view. When it was completed, a commission of the best artists in Florence, including Leonardo da Vinci, was appointed to decide where the statue should be placed. The entrance to the Palazzo Vecchio near the center of government was chosen. Moving the giant

St. Paul *was one of the four statues Michelangelo completed for Pope Pius III in the early 1500s.*

Of all of Michelangelo's sculptures, few are as well known as the David.

A Little Too Nosy

According to Michelangelo biographer Ascanio Condivi in *The Life of Michelangelo*, Piero di Tommaso Soderini, head of the Florentine government, came to see the *David* before it was unveiled to the public. Michelangelo was doing a bit of retouching to the marble when Soderini remarked that the nose was too large. Instead of being angry or insulted, Michelangelo climbed the framework around the statue and using his chisel, he appeared to (but did not) make a change in the nose, causing a bit of marble dust to fall to the ground below. Then he said to Soderini, "Look at it now," and the Florentine ruler replied, "I like it better. You have given it life."[1]

1. Quoted in Ascanio Condivi, "The Life of Michael Angelo Buonarroti" in *Michael Angelo Buonarroti*. Trans. Charles Holroyd. London, UK: Duckworth and Co., 1903, p. 119.

statue, which weighed more than 6 tons (5.44 mt), required a sling-like device to keep it safe and suspended off the ground.

The *David* was considered to be a symbol of the city and its republican government—the underdog, threatened by powerful enemies and tyrants, that ultimately vanquished its foes. Some Medici supporters and those who were offended by the statue's nudity protested, but for the most part, *David* was widely accepted, praised as a great masterpiece, and imitated by other artists at the time.

In Praise of *David*

Poeschke wrote that the *David*'s "athletically developed torso, like its colossal size and nudity, is a direct borrowing from classical sculpture."[24] Michelangelo carved the statue out of a single block of marble without adding any other pieces. Condivi wrote that the statue was "so exactly to size that the old surface of the outsides of the marble may be seen on the top of the head and in the base."[25] Vasari wrote, "The legs are finely turned, the slender flanks divine, and the graceful pose unequalled, while such feet, hands, and head have never been excelled. After seeing this no one need wish to look at any other sculpture or the work of any other artist."[26] Antonio Forcellino called the *David* "the new god of male beauty."[27]

Keeping Busy

While the *David* was a huge project, it was not Michelangelo's only project while he was in Florence. The Guild of Wool Merchants requested full-size sculptures of the 12 apostles for

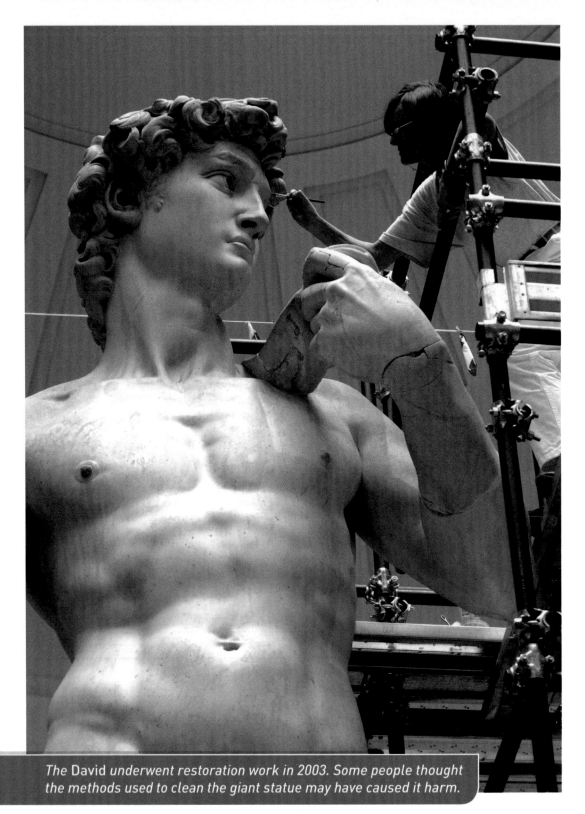

The David underwent restoration work in 2003. Some people thought the methods used to clean the giant statue may have caused it harm.

the cathedral. Michelangelo started to carve them but had so many commissions that all he got done was a half-completed statue of *St. Matthew* in 1506. The contract was annulled, or canceled, and other sculptors completed the remaining apostles. The *St. Matthew* was about 8.8 feet (2.7 m) tall and was a perfect example of the figure freeing itself from the block of marble with the aid of the sculptor. Only the front part of the *St. Matthew* had been carved, showing a powerfully muscled chest and a twisted, moving body emerging out of the stone.

Piero di Tommaso Soderini, the head of the government in Florence, asked Michelangelo to cast a bronze statue of the *David*, which, when completed, was sent to a collector in France, where it was ultimately lost. Then, a wealthy family of Flemish merchants commissioned him to carve the *Madonna of Bruges*, which is 4 feet 2.5 inches (1.28 m) tall. The completed piece was sent to the Church of Notre Dame in Bruges and contributed to Michelangelo's fame and status in northern Europe.

Michelangelo's unfinished St. Matthew *emerges from the marble.*

The Real Michelangelo

Michelangelo was devoted to the arts and loved knowledge. Condivi wrote that, in 1553, "by some he was held to be proud, and by others odd and eccentric."[1] He took pleasure in talking with friends and delighted in reading the philosophers and studying the Old and New Testament of the Bible. "No evil thoughts were born in him," Condivi stated. "He loved not only human beauty, but universally every beautiful thing."[2] Condivi continued,

And as he took little food so he took little sleep, which, as he says, rarely did him any good, for sleeping almost always made his head ache, and too much sleep made his stomach bad. When he was more robust he often slept in his clothes and with his buskins [laced boots] on ... he has sometimes been so long without taking them off that when he did so the skin came off with them like the slough of a snake.[3]

Although Michelangelo enjoyed his privacy, biographer William E. Wallace dispels the myth that the artist was a loner. "You never think of Michelangelo laughing," Wallace wrote. "But he had a wonderful sense of humor ... He liked to laugh. Records show him becoming friendly with a large number of people largely because he just liked to hang out with them."[4]

1. Ascanio Condivi, "The Life of Michelangelo" in *Michael Angelo Buonarroti*. Trans. Charles Holroyd. London, UK: Duckworth and Co., 1903, p. 84.
2. Condivi, "Life of Michelangelo," p. 87.
3. Condivi, "Life of Michelangelo," p. 88.
4. Quoted in Kathleen McGarvey, "Michelangelo Lived Large—and 'Loved to Laugh,'" University of Rochester Newscenter, March 20, 2018. www.rochester.edu/newscenter/michelangelo-lived-large-and-loved-to-laugh-306262/.

A Chance for Confrontation

When Michelangelo returned to Florence in 1501, Florentines were buzzing about the return of the great master Leonardo da Vinci, who, at nearly 50, was almost twice Michelangelo's age. In 1503, Leonardo was commissioned to do a fresco in the government council chamber at the Palazzo Vecchio. His *Battle of Anghiari* focused on the fight over the flag by the cavalry on horseback. However, he never finished the fresco and left Florence for other well-paid commissions in Milan.

In 1504, Michelangelo was assigned to paint *The Battle of Cascina* on the wall across from Leonardo's fresco.

Michelangelo's painting was supposed to capture the surprise attack of enemy troops from Pisa on Florentine foot soldiers bathing and relaxing in the river. Michelangelo finished the preliminary drawing, or cartoon, but never completed the fresco because he was called to Rome by Pope Julius II.

If both Leonardo and Michelangelo had finished the painting phase of their commissions, they might have worked together under the same roof in what art historian James Beck stated "would have been the most spectacular artistic confrontation of the Renaissance."[28]

The Artist and the Pope

What happens when a passionate artist and a determined pope work together? In 1505, the world found out. Cardinal Giuliano della Rovere was named Pope Julius II. He was a man with grand ideas and plans. He wanted to expel foreigners, unify the Papal States, and create a new Rome. To reflect his ideas of art and culture, Julius II brought together architect Donato Bramante, the painter Raphael, the builder Giuliano da Sangallo, and Michelangelo. The work Michelangelo did for this pope would be the masterpiece of his lifetime, but it would also be part of a time of conflict, frustration, and grudging respect.

A significant portion of Michelangelo's life involved his conflict-filled relationship with Julius. Both men were stubborn and willful characters who often butted heads about art projects though they worked together for more than eight years.

An Abandoned Tomb

Michelangelo's first commission from Julius was for his tomb, which was to eventually be placed within St. Peter's Basilica. Michelangelo's plans were for a massive monument of marble, standing detached from the walls, rising into three levels, and tapering into a pyramid at the top. Author Lutz Heusinger described Michelangelo's original plans

Money and Stress

At the same time that Michelangelo was paying workmen for transporting the Carrara marble to Rome for Julius's tomb, he was also being pressured for money by his father and two of his brothers. His brothers wanted Michelangelo to financially back them in a business or find them jobs in Rome. According to art historian John T. Spike in his book *Young Michelangelo: The Path to the Sistine*,

> Michelangelo pushed back firmly, pleading poverty as he always did: "A few days ago I wrote Lodovico and told him that I have four hundred large ducats worth of marble here and that I owe a hundred and forty ducats on it, so that I haven't got a quattrino [penny]. I'm telling you the same thing, so that you may see that for the time being, I cannot help you."[1]

Spike explained that Michelangelo's father knew his son's bank accounts in Florence and Rome were far from empty. He knew that his son lied to him about money as often as he did in return. Despite Michelangelo's wealth, it never seemed enough since, according to Spike, the artist felt constant stress about money. Spike wrote, "He began to ask Julius repeatedly, insistently, obsessively, for more money,"[2] and this resulted in their first major conflict in 1506.

1. John T. Spike, *Young Michelangelo: The Path to the Sistine*. New York, NY: Vendome Press, 2010, p. 198.
2. Spike, *Young Michelangelo*.

for the tomb for which he was to be paid 10,000 ducats over the course of 5 years. According to Heusinger,

> Forty life-size statues were to surround the tomb, which was to be 23 feet (7.01 m) wide, 36 feet, 3 inches (11.05 m) deep, 26 feet, 4 inches (8.03 m) high ... the 'Victories' and the 'Slaves' intended for the lower level ... Moses and St. Paul, among others, were to have been placed in the middle level, surrounded by representations of examples of the active and contemplative lives ... At the summit ... there was to have been a portrayal of two angels leading the Pope out of his tomb on the day of the Last Judgment.[29]

Michelangelo returned to Carrara to choose the marble blocks for the project. He was gone for eight months, and

Some of the world's most beautiful marble is still found in this marble quarry in Carrara.

during that time, the rebuilding of St. Peter's began with Bramante as chief architect. This renovation cost a huge amount of money, and so, Julius II decided to wait on the tomb project for a while.

Unfortunately, Michelangelo did not know this. When more than 90 wagonloads of marble were cut, transported, and unloaded, he went to see Julius II for the money to pay for everything. His Holiness was busy, so Michelangelo paid the workers out of his own pocket, fully expecting to be repaid by the pope soon after. He returned again and again to see the pope, but each time, he was turned away.

Michelangelo got angry. Condivi wrote that the young sculptor left Julius a message, saying, "You may tell the Pope that, henceforward, if he wants me, he must look for me elsewhere."[30] Michelangelo then returned home, told his servants to sell his possessions, and rode off to Florence on horseback.

Frustration and Forgiveness

Julius II sent several messengers to convince Michelangelo to return to Rome, but he responded that since Julius apparently was not continuing with the tomb project, he was free to pursue other assignments. For three months, angry letters were exchanged between the two men, but nothing was resolved.

When the pope came to Florence, Michelangelo feared for his safety. Finally, he agreed to meet with Julius II in the city of Bologna. When he did, he got down on his knees and begged for forgiveness.

Julius pardoned Michelangelo and also assigned him a new commission in Bologna. He wanted a bronze statue of himself, three times larger than life, to watch over (some said threaten) the city. Michelangelo received 1,000 ducats for the statue, which was completed in 1508. (It was torn down and sold for scrap three years later.) Michelangelo returned to Rome, ready to continue work on Julius's tomb, but the pope had a far grander project in mind.

A Rival's Recommendation

Both Condivi and Vasari wrote that the architect Bramante convinced the pope to have Michelangelo paint the giant ceiling of the Vatican's Sistine Chapel, which is the pope's chapel and the place where papal elections are held. Bramante knew that Michelangelo primarily worked with sculptures and that he had little experience in the required style of fresco painting. (Fresco is a type of painting that is done directly on the wet plaster of a wall or ceiling so that the colors penetrate.

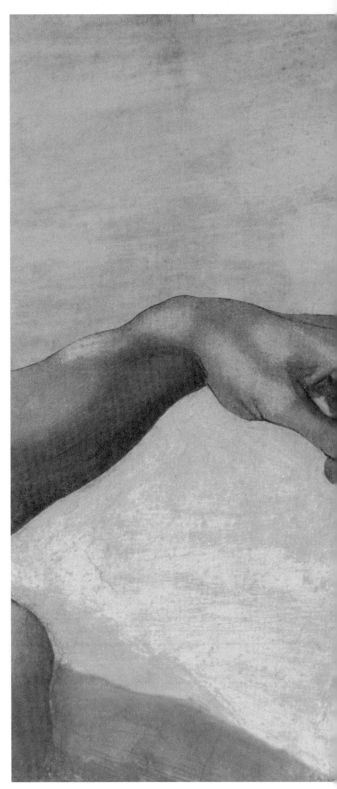

This famous image of God and Adam reaching out to touch fingers is from the ceiling of the Sistine Chapel.

Michelangelo filled more than 12,000 square feet (1,115 sq m) of space when he painted the Sistine Chapel's ceiling, shown here.

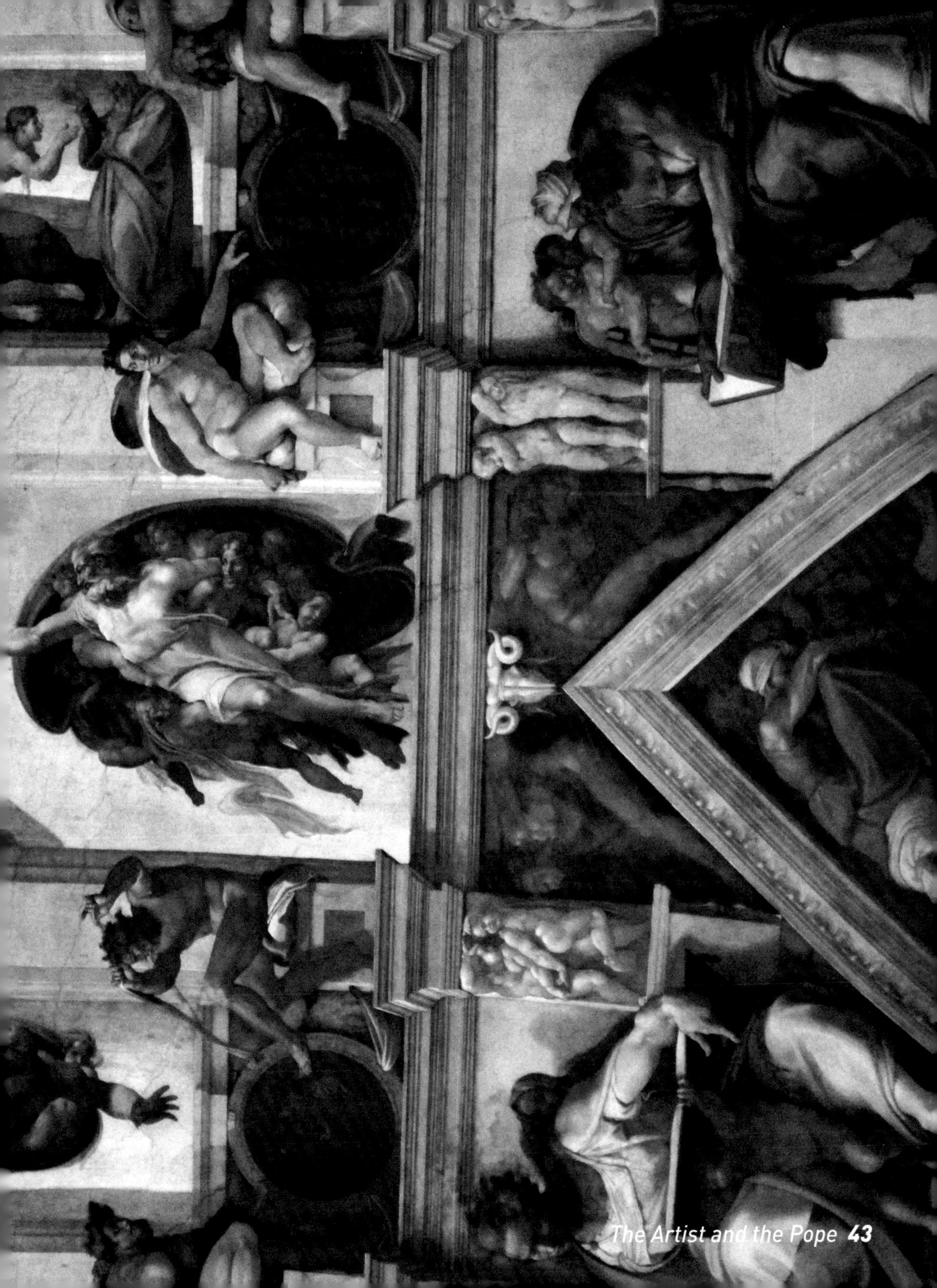

The colors can then be absorbed before the plaster hardens.) This lack of experience was why Bramante recommended Michelangelo. According to Condivi and Vasari, the two men were rivals, and the architect wanted the sculptor to fail.

Michelangelo did everything he could to get out of the Sistine Chapel commission. He insisted he was a sculptor, not a painter. The more Michelangelo tried to escape, the more the pope held onto him. Finally, Michelangelo agreed.

The first step in this monumental project was building scaffolding capable of supporting buckets of water, bags of sand and lime, and several painters 68 feet (20.7 m) above the ground. The chapel was still to be used as a place of worship by the pope and senior officials, so the scaffolding could not block the aisles. According to biographer Ross King, Michelangelo designed "a series of footbridges that spanned the chapel from the level of the windows" using "a number of stepped arches … that served as linked bridges across the void, giving the painters and plasterers decks on which to work as well as access to every part of the ceiling."[31]

Figures Across the Ceiling
It immediately became clear that the pope and Michelangelo had distinctly different plans for the ceiling of the Sistine Chapel. They disagreed about the design, the content, and the size of the work. The pope had planned for the ceiling fresco to feature the 12 Apostles, but Michelangelo wanted much more. When he objected to Julius II, the pope gave him complete freedom to choose his subjects. Michelangelo divided the curved barrel vault of the ceiling into nine well-known scenes from the Old Testament, including the division of light from darkness; the creation of the sun, moon, and planets; the separation of land from the oceans; the creation of Adam and Eve; and the Great Flood. He focused on the human figure with minimal landscape, including what King described as the world-famous "finger-to-finger transmission of the spark of life from God to Adam."[32]

The ceiling also has four large triangular-shaped vaulting pieces called pendentives in each corner between the arches, rounded half-moon spaces above the windows called lunettes, small triangular-shaped spaces above the windows called spandrels, and rectangular panels. Prophets from the Old Testament and sibyls (prophetic women who foretold the future) were painted in the rectangular panels. The lunettes were filled with paintings of ancestors of Jesus, including several women. This depiction of Jesus's female ancestors (other than Mary) was a first in Christian religious art. The large pendentives show scenes of great Jewish figures of the Bible—Moses, Esther, David, and Judith. The triangular-shaped spandrels were all filled with domestic scenes of family life.

Much of the surface of the ceiling was curved, and a painting technique called foreshortening was often utilized. Since the ceiling would be viewed at a distance from the ground or at angles, those parts of figures nearest to the viewers were generally painted larger than those further away to create the illusion of three-dimensional fullness and distance. Throughout the painting, Michelangelo included adult nude figures (*ignudi*) and naked little cupids and angels (*putti*) that appear to hold up, sit on, or pose near various ceiling ornamentation such as medallions, cornices, and moldings. There are also a number of what King described as "a series of grotesque nudes ... smaller in size than the *ignudi*, these two dozen bronze-colored nudes kick, squirm, and scream in confined areas."[33]

Sore Muscles and Hard Work

The Sistine Chapel was an immensely difficult project. Michelangelo made more than 1,000 drawings before he began painting. He did not paint the chapel ceiling while lying flat on his back on the scaffolding, as is commonly believed. Instead, he and his assistants stood upright, bending their necks at various angles to paint. It did not take long for Michelangelo's neck and shoulder muscles to hurt, and even his eyesight was affected. "This posture," George Bull wrote, "left him for a while

unable to read a letter without holding it above his head."[34]

The work on the ceiling took a physical and emotional toll on Michelangelo, who wrote a sonnet about his unhappy experiences to his friend Giovanni di Benedetto from Pistoia, Italy, in 1510:

*I've grown a goitre by dwelling in
    this den—
As cats from stagnant streams
    in Lombardy,
Or in what other land they hap
    to be—
Which drives the belly close
    beneath the chin:
My beard turns up to heaven;
    my nape falls in,
Fixed on my spine: my
    breast-bone visibly
Grows like a harp: a
    rich embroidery
Bedews my face from brush-drops
    thick and thin ...
Come then, Giovanni, try
To succour my dead pictures and
    my fame,
Since foul I fare and painting is
    my shame.*[35]

While Michelangelo worked on the chapel ceiling, Julius often left Rome, traveling to Bologna or Venice in an attempt to rid Italy of certain groups of Europeans. Whenever Julius returned, he visited Michelangelo to see how the work was progressing. The answers he was given were often short.

The Sistine Chapel ceiling is an astounding work of art that amazes those who see it.

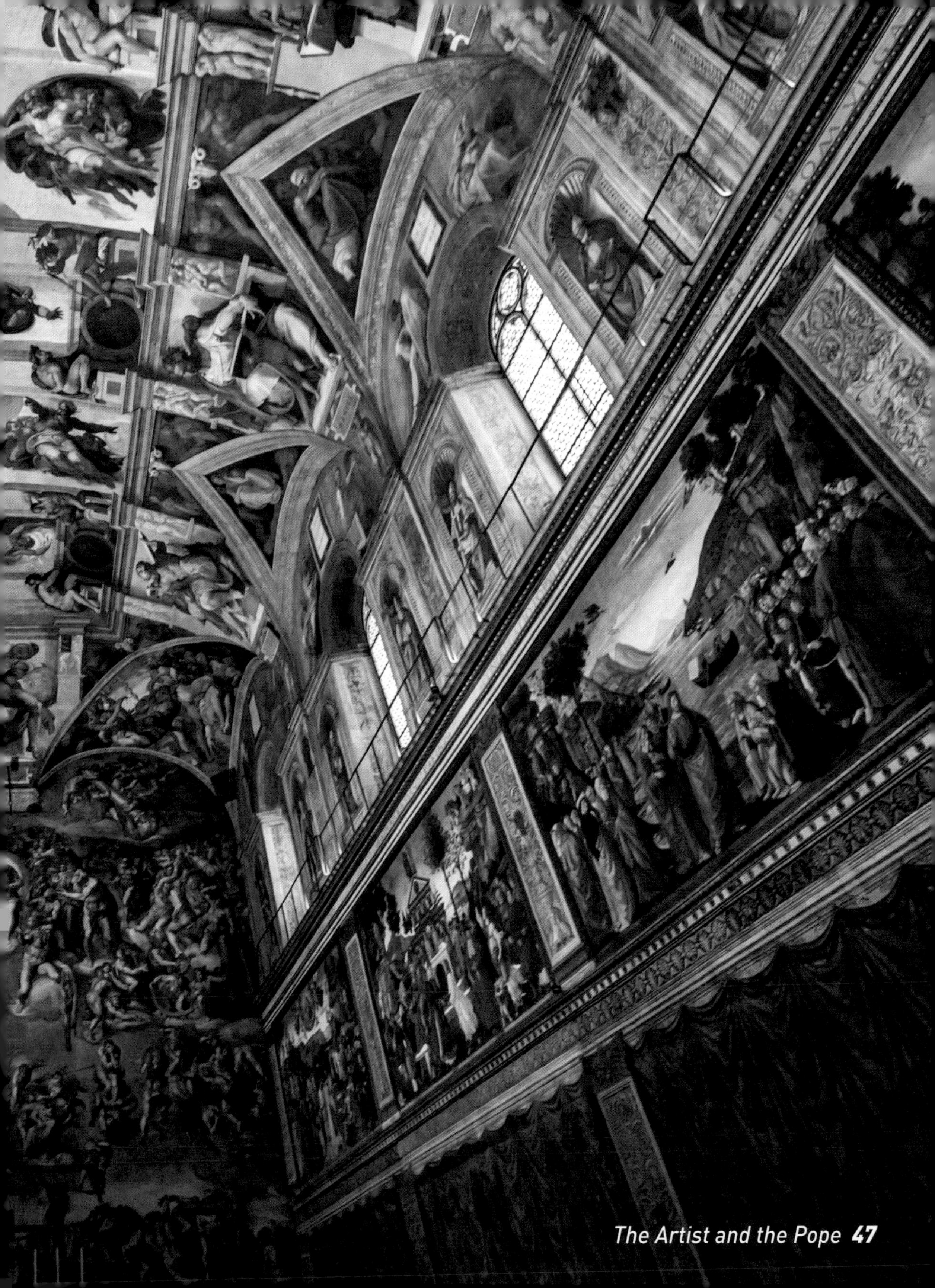

A Modern Sistine Chapel

Inside the Auditorium della Conciliazione, the music swelled, laser lights rippled, dancers and acrobats gyrated, and the images from the Sistine Chapel were projected overhead. Michelangelo's work was being brought to life in 2018 in front of the audience's eyes, and the crowd was mesmerized.

Universal Judgement: Michelangelo and the Secrets of the Sistine Chapel was an incredible multimedia production that carried the Vatican's approval. It opened in Rome in early 2018, and the main musical theme was written by rock legend Sting. It took producer Marco Balich four years to complete the plans for the show—the same amount of time it took Michelangelo to finish the ceiling. Lulu Helbek, codirector of the show, stated that "it's about capturing the spirit between the artist and his masterpiece."[1] Fotis Nikolaou, the show's choreographer, added, "We can't do anything bigger than Michelangelo, it's like committing a sin to suggest that ... It's like saying thank you to a masterpiece like the Sistine Chapel."[2]

1. Quoted in Elisabetta Povoledo, "Bringing the Sistine Chapel to Life, with the Vatican's Blessing," *New York Times*, March 12, 2018. www.nytimes.com/2018/03/12/theater/sistine-chapel-ultimate-judgment.html.
2. Quoted in Povoledo, "Bringing the Sistine Chapel to Life."

One day, when he asked when Michelangelo would finish the ceiling, Michelangelo only replied, "When I can."[36]

Both Condivi and Vasari related an incident that occurred when Michelangelo asked the pope if he could go home to Florence to spend the feast of St. John with his family and requested money for his journey. Again, the pope asked, "When will this chapel be ready?" and Michelangelo again replied, "When I can get it done, Holy Father." Vasari wrote,

The Pope struck him with his mace [staff], repeating, "When I can, when I can, I will make you finish it!" Michelangelo, however, returned to his house to prepare for his journey to Florence, when the Pope sent Cursio, his chamberlain, with five hundred scudi to appease him and excuse the Pope ... As Michelangelo knew the Pope, and was really devoted to him, he laughed, especially as such things always turned to his advantage, and the Pope did everything to retain his goodwill.[37]

Open to the Public

When Michelangelo completed half of the ceiling, he took the scaffolding down and, at the request of the pope, opened up the chapel to the public. Many people came to view the half-finished masterpiece. Michelangelo put the scaffolding back up and completed the remaining parts of the ceiling in 20 months, often working nights by candlelight. The more than 340 figures painted on the second half of the ceiling were larger and painted in unusually bright yellows, greens, oranges, blues, reds, and whites.

All of Italy was following the work of Michelangelo. Wealthy art lovers and collectors would climb the scaffolding to visit and chat. Many visitors were so impressed by Michelangelo's talent that they discussed future commissions with him.

In July 1512, Michelangelo wrote to his brother Buonarroto, "I toil harder than any man who ever was, unwell and with enormous effort; and yet I have the patience to reach the desired end."[38] Another letter written to his father in October 1512 was full of self-pity. Michelangelo complained, "I lead a miserable existence ... I live wearied by stupendous labours and beset by a thousand anxieties. And thus have I lived for some fifteen years now and never an hour's happiness have I had, and all this I have done in order to help you, though you have never either recognized or believed it."[39]

The Sistine Chapel ceiling was finally completed on October 31, 1512, four years and four weeks after Michelangelo first began. Early 19th-century German author Johann Wolfgang von Goethe wrote, "Until you have seen the Sistine Chapel, you can have no adequate conception of what man is capable of accomplishing."[40] Forcellino wrote, "What Michelangelo had achieved with the statue of David not ten years earlier was now repeated, with the painting of the chapel ceiling creating an even greater sensation. At the age of thirty-seven, the ambitious Florentine had become a living legend."[41]

In February 1513, four months after the unveiling of the ceiling, Pope Julius II died. Before his death, Julius made it clear to his heirs and family that he wished Michelangelo to continue work on his tomb and issued a papal bull, or public order, allocating funds for the tomb.

Michelangelo and Julius's executors signed a contract increasing the artist's payment. They agreed the tomb would be completed in seven years but would be attached to a wall of St. Peter's Basilica instead of freestanding. Michelangelo was eager to return to what he believed was his primary talent—working as a sculptor.

Even seated, Michelangelo's Moses is more than 8 feet (2.4 m) tall and shows great personality and emotion.

A Tragic Tomb

At last, the white marble that had been gathering dust for years was brought to Michelangelo's workshop. He began carving several statues, including the *Moses*, the *Dying Slave*, and the *Rebellious Slave*. He was interrupted by the newly elected pope, Cardinal Giovanni de' Medici, who took the name of Leo X in March 1513. Giovanni had been a childhood friend of Michelangelo, and he was a patron of the arts who supported the artist.

Over the next 32 years, the renowned artist kept trying to work on Julius's tomb but was repeatedly called away by various popes to work on other commissions. Five additional contracts were modified and signed by Julius's heirs, and each time, the size of the tomb was reduced. Then, the Rovere heirs decided to sue Michelangelo for the money they had already paid him. A negotiated settlement was reached, and still another contract was signed. The tomb was decreased even further in size, and it was agreed that it should be placed in the Church of San Pietro in Vincoli, where Julius II had served as cardinal, instead of in St. Peter's Basilica.

Several popes intervened to excuse Michelangelo from working on the tomb until the Rovere family ultimately agreed, in a 1542 contract, to a simple tomb with only a fraction of the originally planned statues. The *Dying Slave* and *Rebellious Slave* were not placed on the tomb. After passing through private hands, the two statues are now on exhibit in the Louvre in Paris.

In 1542, an older, more spiritual Michelangelo sculpted figures of biblical heroines Rachel and Leah. Art historians believe the two represented faith and good works, or as Vasari and Condivi note, the active life and the contemplative life. These two figures replaced the slave figures on the tomb of Julius, and historians differ as to whether Michelangelo or another sculptor completed the figures.

The central statue of Moses was described by art historian and restorer Umberto Baldini as having "enormous strength … [a] robust fluctuating play of lights and shadows."[42] Condivi noted the face of Moses is both tender and terrifying, while Vasari referred to it as being holy and formidable. Moses holds the tablets of the law under one arm and his flowing beard in the fingers of his other hand.

The completed structure was finally unveiled at the Church of San Pietro in 1545, nearly 40 years after its inception. It was beautiful, but to many art historians, it was also tragic since its size was so drastically reduced from Michelangelo's original plans and he had such a small role in its final form. The artist had little time to dwell on his creation, however, because there was a new pope in Rome, and he too was interested in the arts.

CHAPTER FOUR

The Medicis and Michelangelo

Despite the childhood connection between Leo X and Michelangelo, the two men were often at odds. The pope respected the artist's talent, but not his temperament. He told another painter in confidence that "Michelangelo is frightening ... one cannot deal with him."[43] Michelangelo retaliated by painting a number of caricatures of Leo X and his cousin. Even though there was tension between Leo X and Michelangelo, the pope had a new project in mind for his childhood friend.

Another Abandoned Project

As the first Florentine pope, Leo X focused his artistic aspirations on his home city and powerful family rather than on the Vatican in Rome. In 1516, he commissioned Michelangelo to design and complete the facade (front wall) of the Basilica of San Lorenzo in Florence. Michelangelo agreed to complete the project in eight years. George Bull wrote, "The work ... included eight fluted marble columns rising to the first cornice and framing the three doors of the church and a total of twenty-two statues, of which the six on the storey over the door were to be over life-size seated figures in bronze ... and seven marble scenes in low relief, five square panels and two round."[44]

Michelangelo traveled to Carrara to pick out the marble for the new project, but while he was there, he received

Pope Leo X, shown here in this painting by Raphael, was known for forgiving sins in order to receive more donations to the church.

a letter from the pope insisting that he get his marble in the Pietrasanta Mountains, near Seravezza, Italy. Michelangelo believed it was too difficult and expensive to get to this new site but had little choice. A road had to be built several miles through the mountains to get there. Bad weather, inexperienced marble cutters and quarrymen, and accidents with the marble blocks caused numerous delays.

One particular incident occurred in the spring, "when an iron fastening broke and a fine column of marble fell and shattered, nearly killing Michelangelo and several others. Again, Michelangelo noted that he was the victim of bad, dishonest workmanship."[45] Finally, in 1520, Leo canceled the entire project.

Michelangelo was shocked and upset at losing the commission and wrote a letter, according to Bull, to a lawyer or legal clerk in Florence to set the record straight and account for the money he had already spent on the facade. He wrote,

> I have ... not charg[ed] to Pope Leo ... for the wooden model for the said façade, which I sent to Rome; nor am I putting to his account the period of three years that I have lost over this; nor am I putting to his account that I have been ruined over the said work of San Lorenzo; nor am I putting

> to his account the gross insult of having brought me here to do the said work, and then taking it from me; ... nor do I charge to his account my house in Rome that I have left, including marble, furniture and completed work, which has deteriorated to the amount of over 500 ducats.[46]

With the Vatican short of cash and fighting the French in northern Italy and Milan, the pope gave church members the chance to reduce their punishment for sins by contributing to the church, a process known as "selling indulgences." In addition, those who made the most generous donations were given positions within the church.

From One Pope to the Next

When 45-year-old Pope Leo X's brother Giuliano and nephew Lorenzo died (in 1516 and 1519 respectively), he suddenly became far more aware of his own mortality. He asked Michelangelo to begin an art project designed to glorify the Medici family. A new sacristy, Medici tomb, and library became the top priorities. The library would contain the late Lorenzo the Magnificent's collection of rare books, statues, and letters. The tomb would hold the remains of Lorenzo, who had died in 1492; Lorenzo's brother Giuliano, who was murdered in 1478; and Leo's brother and nephew.

Michelangelo began designing the Medici tomb, but then, Leo died suddenly in early 1521, just before turning 46. His replacement, Adrian VI of the Netherlands (also known as Hadrian), was not at all interested in art or Michelangelo. Adrian was careful with finances and tried to limit Medici power. Michelangelo resumed working on the tomb of Julius. However, Adrian's term as pope was a brief one, as he died less than two years after becoming pope. He was succeeded by Florentine Cardinal Giulio de' Medici, who took the name Clement VII. William E. Wallace wrote, "Adrian's passing ... was accompanied by a collective sigh of relief, especially from the artists who had enjoyed Leo X's liberality."[47]

"Impetuosity and Fury"

The new pope shifted Michelangelo away from working on Julius's tomb to building and sculpting Medici projects. In 1525, 50-year-old Michelangelo worked simultaneously on the chapel and library and supervised a workforce of more than 100 stonecutters and carvers.

Michelangelo introduced various aspects of Mannerism, a style of art that emphasized exaggerated twists and distortions of the human body over balance or symmetry. He incorporated Mannerist characteristics into his sculptures and architecture, varying perspective and using columns built into the walls that often extended over several stories. Michelangelo sculpted more than six statues at a time, going from one to the other. Frequently, after a 14-hour workday, the artist worked into the night by candlelight. His only day of rest was Sunday, when he visited his father and brothers in Florence. Wallace quotes Blaise de Vignère, a Frenchman who described watching Michelangelo later in life at work on a statue:

I have seen Michelangelo, although more than sixty years old and no longer among the most robust, knock off more chips of a very hard marble in a quarter of an hour than three young stone carvers could have done in three or four, an almost incredible thing to one who has not seen it; and I thought the whole work would fall to pieces because he moved with such impetuosity and fury, knocking to the floor large chunks three and four fingers thick with a single blow so precisely aimed that if he had gone even minimally further than necessary, he risked losing it all.[48]

Time and Serenity

Michelangelo's original concept for the Medici Chapel called for four tombs, many statues, and much ornamentation. The tomb he finally completed after several years was unfinished but is still considered one of his masterpieces. According to

The lobby of the Laurentian Library, designed by Michelangelo, is dominated by a triple staircase that fills more than half the chamber.

Wallace, "The two Medici dukes ... [Lorenzo and Guiliano] ... are seated in shallow niches above the sarcophagi that contain their remains ... Four nude allegorical figures recline on the curved sarcophagi lids. Traditionally these represent Day and Night, Dawn and Dusk—a sort of figural meditation on time."[49] The Medici Chapel artwork focused on the consistent and unstoppable passage of time and the shortness of human life.

The Laurentian Library was built in the same Basilica of San Lorenzo complex as the chapel to house the books and manuscripts of the Medicis. The library's lobby is one of the most beautiful and impressive of Michelangelo's architectural works. "This is an entire room," Wallace wrote, "devoted to the transitional experience of moving from the noisy exterior to the quiet serenity of the library."[50] The staircases lead into the reading room by means of a central, wide aisle, flanked on both sides by beautiful wooden reading desks and carved wooden ceiling panels. There are two desks to each large stone-framed window, permitting abundant light to study the rare items in the library. "To sit at one of the carved walnut desks," Wallace wrote, "is to become a part of the building."[51]

Changing Leaders

For years, France and Spain fought for control of Italy, with Spain the ultimate victor. Pope Clement united with leaders from France, England, Venice, Milan, and Florence to form the League of Cognac, but they were no match for the Spanish troops.

Spain's imperial soldiers had not been paid and were frustrated, so they persuaded their commanders to march southward toward Rome, destroying and looting all towns along the way. The imperial army was made up of Spanish and German soldiers, most of them angry Lutherans who wanted revenge against the papacy in Rome and to steal the riches of the Eternal City. The troops entered Rome on May 6, 1527, and a brutal battle followed, in which Clement was taken prisoner.

When the citizens of Florence learned what had happened in Rome, they rose up on May 16, forcing the Medicis out of the city and reestablishing the Florentine Republic. After seven months of captivity, Clement agreed to work for peace, reform the church, and accept the new Lutheran faith of the Reformation, and he was restored to power. Clement and Charles V signed a treaty, stating that the pope would crown the Holy Roman emperor in a public ceremony and give him control of Naples. Charles V hoped this would demonstrate the pope's deference to him and convince the pope's followers to accept Charles V's authority. In return, Charles V agreed to restore the Medicis' rule in Florence.

After crowing Charles V as Holy Roman emperor in February 1530, the pope returned to Florence to exact revenge on those who had ousted the Medicis. One of those who had supported the republic was Michelangelo, who had cut back his work on the Medici commissions during that uncertain time period. Wallace wrote,

Despite Clement's effort to dissuade him, Michelangelo elected to side with his native city, because, above all, he was a Florentine with deeply republican loyalties. In Florence's hour of need, he was appointed director of the city's fortifications, and thus he now devoted himself to resisting the very man who had been his pope, patron, and strongest supporter during the previous ten years.[52]

Torn Between Allegiances

As the Florentine Republic prepared themselves to battle the troops of the Holy Roman emperor and the papal forces of Clement, Michelangelo found himself in an entirely different role. He was named governor-general of the city's fortifications. He sat on Florence's governing council and as Bull wrote, "around the hill of San Miniato, rising high over Florence and commanding a broad sweep of countryside to the south-east beyond the Arno, he was throwing a circle of huge earthworks to support the artillery needed to halt the enemy and bombard its siegeworks."[53] Michelangelo used the church's tall bell tower as a lookout point and built elevated artillery platforms. He used cannons, defensive walls, and angular structures in the city's defenses. He also ordered bales of wool and heavy mattresses suspended by ropes to protect the bell tower from enemy cannon fire.

After he had completed the tasks of fortifying the city, Michelangelo secretly fled to Venice. He feared for his life from those who did not like his close associations with the Medicis. He changed his mind shortly after and returned to Florence, staying throughout the bloody siege. The republic was cut off from food and supplies for many months, and many died from

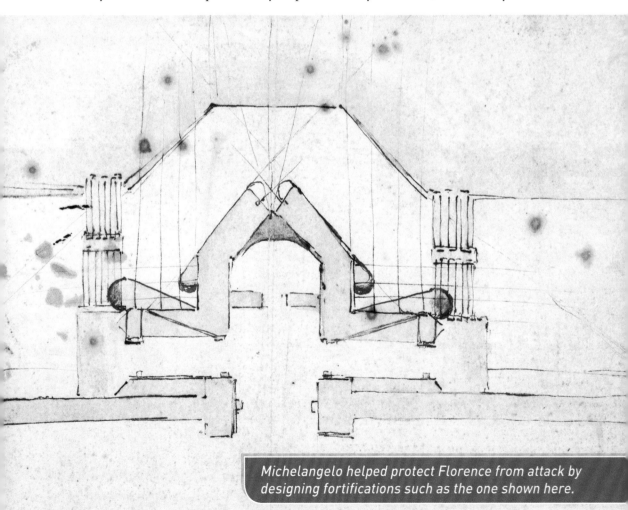

Michelangelo helped protect Florence from attack by designing fortifications such as the one shown here.

disease and hunger. After seven months, an agreement was reached between Florentine emissaries, Clement, and Charles V. The Medicis took control of the city and set out to punish those who had opposed their family rule.

Michelangelo was in a difficult situation and quickly went into hiding. Those in favor of the republic distrusted him because he had temporarily fled the city and had never cut his Medici connections entirely. The Medicis were unhappy because he had supported the republic and worked on the city's fortifications against them. He was particularly hated by Florence's new governor, Alessandro de' Medici. The governor considered Michelangelo a traitor and ordered his execution. Clement, however, did not want any harm to come to Michelangelo. By the end of 1530, the artist was pardoned, was set free, and returned to his work at San Lorenzo, with the pope intervening on his behalf to hold the Rovere heirs at bay in the Julius II tomb contract.

A Time of Loss

During the summer of 1528, the plague struck Florence. Michelangelo lost his beloved brother Buonarroto. Soon after, the artist's 87-year-old father also passed away.

Michelangelo grieved strongly for his lost family members. In 1531, the artist grew ill from working too hard without proper rest or diet. The pope ordered him to cut back on all work except the Medici projects until his health improved. A poem written by Michelangelo about the deaths of his brother and father reveals his deep grief:

> Deep grief such woe unto my
>   heart did give,
> I thought it wept the bitter
>   pain away,
> And tears and moans would let
>   my spirit live.
>
> But fate renews the fount of
>   grief to-day,
> And feeds each hidden root and
>   secret vein
> By death that doth still harder
>   burden lay.
>
> I of thy parting speak; and
>   yet again
> For him, of thee who later left
>   me here,
> My tongue and pen shall speak
>   the separate pain.
>
> He was my brother, thou our
>   father dear;
> Love clung to him and duty
>   bound to thee,
> Nor can I tell which loss I hold
>   most near.[54]

In 1532, while on a trip to Rome to sign yet another Rovere contract concerning the tomb of Julius, the 57-year-old artist (an old man by the standard of the times) met the handsome, intelligent, and charming 23-year-old Tommaso de' Cavalieri. The two remained close friends for the rest of Michelangelo's life. While in Rome, Michelangelo met with Clement twice to discuss painting a fresco for the huge altar wall of the Sistine Chapel. The pope wanted a painting of the day of the Last Judgment, which is the day of Christ's Second Coming according to Christian tradition.

When Clement died in September 1534, Michelangelo lost his last ally among the Medicis and decided to leave Florence permanently. In 1534, he went to Rome to continue Clement's project and spend time with his newfound friend Cavalieri. He cared so deeply for the young man that he not only drew complex, elegant drawings for him but also presented him with multiple letters and poems. The drawings that Michelangelo produced during this time period were unlike anything he had previously done. Stephanie Buck, curator of London's Courtauld Gallery where Michelangelo's drawings were on display in 2010, stated, "These extremely complex and beautiful works show Michelangelo's power of invention, the immense creativity, and mastery in the medium. They also show him engaged with concepts of love and beauty."[55]

CHAPTER FIVE

At His Peak

When Michelangelo returned to Rome in 1534, he was 59 years old and at the peak of his career, surrounded by people who liked and admired him. The new pope, Paul III (born Alessandro Farnese), was anxious for him to begin work on *The Last Judgment*. The space for this painting was huge, measuring around 2,100 square feet (195 sq m). The completed painting took six years to finish.

Changed Man, Changed World

Paul III declared Michelangelo as the main paid architect, painter, and sculptor for the Apostolic Palace, or official residence of the pope at the Vatican. As he was immersed in the Sistine Chapel's fresco of *The Last Judgment*, his paintings from two decades earlier reminded him of how much he and the world had changed over those years. The chapel ceiling was composed of separate scenes with a particular point of view, but *The Last Judgment* was one huge scene with the single theme of divine punishment, or resurrection and salvation. The Roman Catholic Church was dominant and unchallenged when the ceiling was first painted, and now there was the Protestant Reformation and the church's response to Protestantism, the Counter-Reformation.

Michelangelo's The Last Judgment *takes up the entire wall behind the altar of the Sistine Chapel. The painting contains more than 300 figures awaiting the judgment of Christ.*

A Moment of Gloom and Terror

The style used in *The Last Judgment* reflected the changes in the culture's religious thinking, as well as in Michelangelo's talents and spiritual beliefs. While the paintings on the Sistine Chapel's ceiling were beautiful and joyful, the fresco was full of gloom and terror. It was divided into three main rows of figures. The top row was heaven with the figures of Jesus, the Virgin Mary, and saints, prophets, martyrs, and apostles. The middle row was filled with trumpet-blowing angels that were in charge of which souls ascended to heaven or descended to hell. In the bottom row, souls were transported to hell or resurrected. The main figure was Christ, who is, as Antonio Forcellino wrote, "in the act of rising to his feet, drawn along by the gesture of his arm, which sets off a whole vortex of surrounding figures. As a result of this motion, the damned are cast downwards and the saved are propelled upwards, while the ranks of the elect, saints and martyrs … surround Christ."[56] According to Wallace, "In the lower left of the vast fresco, we see the dead issuing forth from graves … The reborn bodies are physically assisted in their ascent to heaven by angels … just as, on the opposite side of the fresco, the damned are violently thrust into hell."[57]

Michelangelo focused on every possible movement, contortion, physical characteristic, gesture, and emotion of the nude human body in *The Last Judgment*, including cruelty, greed, evil, fear, virtue, forgiveness, charity, and joy. A papal official, Biagio da Cesena, criticized the painting, and, according to Giorgio Vasari, "said it was a disgrace to have put so many nudes in such a place, and that the work was better suited to a bathing-place or an inn than a chapel."[58] That remark made Michelangelo so angry he painted Biagio's likeness onto Minos, judge of souls in hell, with a snake wrapped around his body. Along with Biagio's likeness, Michelangelo painted his own face on the skin St. Bartholomew holds. St. Bartholomew had his skin removed as punishment for not renouncing his faith. For St. Sebastian, it is believed that he used Tommaso de' Cavalieri's likeness.

"The Beauty of Man"

On December 25, 1541, the public was invited to see *The Last Judgment* for the first time. People were awed by Michelangelo's vision of the day of judgment, damnation, and resurrection. Fellow artists

Christ's figure is a bit larger than the other figures in The Last Judgement, *most likely to emphasize his importance and power.*

and students praised the immense talent involved in the fresco. Soon, copies, prints, reproductions, and woodcuts were circulating everywhere. However, the most pious church members were shocked by what they considered the inappropriate nudity of holy men and women.

Although the nude figures in his fresco upset some people, Michelangelo felt the human body was beautiful and a testament to God's work. "The perfect beauty of the anatomies and the affecting restraint of the gestures immediately define this painting as the most beautiful and unrepeatable work of art produced in Christendom," Forcellino wrote. "But with equal suddenness, it also attracted criticisms of the artist for its obscenity and lack of faith—for the nudes and the representation of saints and angels as human beings." Forcellino wrote that

Michelangelo believed that "the beauty of Man ... is a product of the greatness of God, and it is impossible to glorify God without showing it."[59]

Saul and St. Peter

The last paintings that Michelangelo would ever paint were for Paul III's Pauline Chapel, not far from the Vatican. Paul III asked Michelangelo to paint two frescoes on the side walls so his chapel would also be remembered by future generations. One fresco was to depict the conversion of Saul and the other the crucifixion of St. Peter.

Michelangelo was now in his mid-70s, which was quite elderly for this era in history, and he worked rather slowly on these two paintings for eight years. The great artist was still sharp and productive, having outlived many of his peers.

A Glimpse of the Artist

Between 2004 and 2009, the Vatican spent more than 3 million euros (around $3.5 million) to restore Michelangelo's frescos located inside the Pauline Chapel. As they worked on *The Crucifixion of St. Peter*, the restorers found something remarkable: a self-portrait of the artist. "It's an extraordinary and moving discovery," stated Maurizio de Luca, the Vatican's chief restorer. "The self-portrait is one of three knights on the left-hand top corner of the fresco who wears a lapis lazuli blue turban. His features are very similar to other known portraits of Michelangelo."[1] Although this was not the first time the artist had added his image to one of his paintings, it was one that had escaped attention until the fresco's restoration.

1. Quoted in Nick Squires, "Michelangelo Signed Fresco with Self-Portrait," *Telegraph*, July 2, 2009. www.telegraph.co.uk/culture/art/art-news/5715571/Michelangelo-signed-fresco-with-self-portrait.html.

The Conversion of Saul is flooded with direct, natural sunlight, which adds to the effect of the painting. Wallace wrote, "Descending as a bolt of lightning from heaven … Christ causes Saul … to fall from his horse, which is now leaping in terror into the background."[60]

In contrast to *The Conversion of Saul*, *The Crucifixion of St. Peter* has little natural light focused on it. In the painting, Peter is shown becoming a heroic martyr by being crucified upside down by the Romans. He lifts his head and glares out of the painting as the soldiers attempt to rotate the cross and drop it into the freshly dug hole in the ground.

Bull believes that Michelangelo's frescoes in the Pauline Chapel illustrate "mankind's dependence for salvation on faith in Christ's power and grace."[61] Questions of faith and salvation were very much on Michelangelo's mind in the last years of his life.

Remodels and Facades

While working on the Pauline Chapel paintings, Michelangelo also took on architectural projects for Paul III. He designed and supervised the building of the third story and the cornice (projecting ledge) of the Farnese Palace, Paul III's family's palace. Instead of continuing the classical style of the first two floors, Michelangelo expanded the windows and raised the ceilings in the new Mannerist style. The pope also commissioned the aging Michelangelo to remodel the Piazza del Campidoglio, Rome's civic center on Capitoline Hill. The original work was planned during the late 1530s and was meant to impress the Holy Roman emperor Charles V

Today, Michelangelo's cordonata is a popular tourist destination.

A Moment's Rage

Michelangelo worked on a personal pietà, which historians believe was meant to decorate his own tomb. From one single block of marble, he sculpted four figures. According to art history professor Joachim Poeschke in his book *Michelangelo and His World*, the figures were linked "by the heavy, sinking figure of Christ, which is only held upright by the support of the three living figures,"[1] the Virgin Mary, Mary Magdalene, and Nicodemus. "Sculpting four figures in a single block—moreover ones not aligned on the same plane—was a challenge that no Italian sculptor had previously attempted," wrote art conservator and Michelangelo expert Antonio Forcellino in his book *Michelangelo: A Tormented Life*. "The figure of Nicodemus is a self-portrait of Michelangelo ... [who] wished to signify his very deep involvement in the worship of Christ, the instrument of mankind's salvation."[2]

In the late 1550s, Michelangelo was truly struggling. A friend had died, another had been imprisoned, and Pope Paul IV had a vendetta against him. Frustrated, the artist lost his temper and in a fit of rage, smashed his pietà with a heavy hammer, shattering part of Jesus's left leg, collarbone, and left arm. Forcellino wrote, "The sculpture remained permanently mutilated, a symbol of a tormented conscience and an uncontrollable anger ... The damage he inflicted on it could be compared to killing one's own offspring."[3] Biographer Giorgio Vasari in *The Life of Michelangelo* wrote that there was a defective vein in the marble, and the sculpture was abandoned. However, Forcellino believes that rage and misery fueled this outbreak, not a flaw in the marble. Michelangelo gave what remained of the pietà to his friend Francesco Bandini, who hired another sculptor to repair it, though he was unsuccessful. This piece still survives today and was previously exhibited at the Museo dell'Opera del Duomo in Florence.

1. Joachim Poeschke, *Michelangelo and His World: Sculpture of the Italian Renaissance*. New York, NY: Harry N. Abrams, 1996, p. 120.
2. Antonio Forcellino, *Michelangelo: A Tormented Life*. Cambridge, UK: Polity, 2010, pp. 287–288.
3. Forcellino, *Michelangelo*, pp. 289–290.

when he visited Rome. However, the project was unfinished for many years.

The bronze equestrian statue of Emperor Marcus Aurelius was moved to the site's center, and Michelangelo carved a new pedestal for it. Around the statue, in the central courtyard, he proposed three buildings. New facades were planned for two of the existing buildings: the Senate Palace, home of the Roman Senate, and the Palace of the Conservators, seat of the city government. A new building, the New Palace, was designed opposite the Palace of the Conservators to match the new facades of the other buildings.

Michelangelo also created a massive ramped staircase called the *cordonata*, which stretched from the bottom of the hill to the main courtyard at the top of the hill. The steps were gently sloped and built wide to allow horses and carriages to easily use them. The bottom of the staircase was flanked by two black granite Egyptian lions. At the top were two large statues of Castor and Pollux, legendary protectors of Rome in the fifth century BC. The *cordonata* and the statue of Marcus Aurelius were the only works completed at the time of Michelangelo's death. The Campidoglio design by Michelangelo is considered to be one of the first civic planning projects built around a central monument and was often imitated by architects in later years.

Working for God

In late 1546, Paul III appointed Michelangelo chief architect to repair the deteriorating buildings of St. Peter's Basilica in Rome. The original church was more than 1,000 years old and was the site where St. Peter was buried.

Michelangelo was 71 years old and had been very ill the previous year. Against his will, he accepted the pope's appointment. Michelangelo wrote to his nephew Lionardo Buonarroti, "Many believe—and I believe—that I have been designated for this work by God. In spite of my old age, I do not want to give it up; I work out of love for God and I put all my hope in Him."[62] St. Peter's became his top priority for the remainder of his life.

Rebuilding the new basilica had first begun under Pope Julius II with architect Donato Bramante while Michelangelo was painting the Sistine Chapel ceiling. Although Bramante was an excellent designer, he was an average engineer and, as Wallace noted, "seriously impaired the structural integrity of the new church."[63] Bramante died in 1514, and many other architects unsuccessfully attempted to add or improve upon the original design. Over the years, the lack of funds often brought the project to a standstill.

Restoring and Simplifying

Michelangelo restored Bramante's original architectural plan for St. Peter's Basilica and simplified it. He destroyed most of the construction added on since 1514, despite opposition from competitors. Then, he designed the beautiful dome of St. Peter's based on Bramante's original concept and Florence's cathedral dome that had been built by Filippo Brunelleschi. Michelangelo focused on the light and included twice as many windows as previous architects had. Forcellino wrote that "this use of light can undoubtedly be explained by Michelangelo's religious feelings, since he interpreted the clear and direct light as the emanation of the divine spirit that calls the faithful to Christ."[64]

Wallace wrote, "From ground to lantern, the building rises in one continuous sweep ... The solid mass and complex surface of St. Peter's exterior contrasts

The dome of St. Peter's Basilica rises about 450 feet (137 m) from the ground and contains intricate, astounding artwork.

with the spacious, luminous interior ... At the center of the immense building is the grave of Saint Peter, and over this venerated spot soars the majestic, light-filled dome."[65]

The new St. Peter's was completed long after the death of Michelangelo. The great artist, however, ensured the continuation and accurate implementation of his original plans for the structure by on-site supervision of the work and written instructions. "The power of his conception transcends the earthly end of its author," Baldini wrote. "Those who came later could not but follow his indications ... Michelangelo's instructions were followed faithfully for decades."[66] According to Forcellino, St. Peter's had become a symbol of Michelangelo's mortality and his quest for salvation and redemption by God.

A Change of Popes

When Paul III died in 1549, Michelangelo lost a friend, admirer, and great patron. Paul III was succeeded by another Buonarroti supporter, Cardinal Giovanni Maria Ciocchi del Monte who took the name of Julius III. The new pope continued to support Michelangelo as chief architect of St. Peter's, defended him from his critics, and sought his thoughts and judgment on any new art projects he considered. Under the new pope, Romans grew suspicious and frightened. This was due, in part, to the role of Cardinal Gian Pietro Carafa.

As part of the Inquisitional Tribunal, Carafa's main goal was opposing whatever he perceived as heresy. He rooted out deviation from the church's teachings, in any form, by the arrest, questioning, and even torture of heretics. Carafa criticized the nudity in *The Last Judgment* and challenged Michelangelo's decisions as St. Peter's chief architect, but the esteemed artist was safely under the pope's protection.

When Julius III died after a sudden illness and fever in 1555, he was replaced by Marcello Cervino, or Marcellus II. Marcellus II supported church reform, but he died of a stroke after only 22 days in office. He was succeeded by Carafa. On the first day of his papacy, Carafa, who took the name Paul IV, suspended all monetary payments to Michelangelo for his work as chief architect. However, throughout all of this, Michelangelo would not leave St. Peter's.

A Fanatical Leader

The new pope's campaign against heretics bordered on the fanatical. He forced all Jewish people to live in a Roman ghetto, locking them in at night. He required Jewish men to wear yellow hats, and Jewish women to wear veils or shawls. The pope declared that all Jewish people were condemned by God to slavery. He banned and burned books that contained what he considered heresy and imprisoned Cardinal Giovanni

Fame and Loss

Michelangelo's worldwide fame protected him from powerful adversaries like Pope Paul IV and others. The 75-year-old artist was internationally famous in 1550 when Giorgio Vasari's book *Lives of the Most Eminent Painters, Sculptors, and Architects* was published (which featured Michelangelo), and it further enhanced his celebrity. Ascanio Condivi's biography, *The Life of Michelangelo*, was printed in 1553 to correct the mistakes of Vasari's book, and a revised edition by Vasari was published in 1568. According to Antonio Forcellino, "Michelangelo was now receiving letters from the King of France, Queen Catherine [Caterina de' Medici], Duke Cosimo, and numerous cardinals who approached him with the same manners they would have adopted with their peers."[1]

The mid-1550s were sad years for Michelangelo. His brother Gismondo—the artist's last living family member—died in 1555. Buonarroto's children were Michelangelo's only heirs, and several had died in childhood. His main beneficiary was his nephew Lionardo, who still resided in Florence. Michelangelo's friend and longtime household assistant, Urbino, died in 1555. Urbino's wife, Cornelia, and young son, also named Michelangelo, lived in Michelangelo's household with him while Urbino was alive. They soon left, but Michelangelo was never alone. In addition to a male assistant, he employed one or two female housekeepers at all times.

1. Antonio Forcellino, *Michelangelo: A Tormented Life*. Cambridge, UK: Polity, 2010, p. 278.

Morone, Michelangelo's close friend and spiritual adviser. The work at St. Peter's came almost completely to a halt, although the pope did not change any of Michelangelo's designs. Vasari noted that the pope was in favor of covering the private parts of figures in *The Last Judgment* and the nudity of angels in *The Conversion of Saul* and *The Crucifixion of St. Peter.* Under Paul IV's papacy, Michelangelo's earnings were reduced to a trickle.

In the late 1550s, Michelangelo designed a church in Rome for Florentine exiles who resided in the city—San Giovanni dei Fiorentini. In 1557, the aged artist actually left Rome for a short time, believing that Spanish troops were about to occupy the Holy City. A settlement was reached, but Michelangelo still enjoyed his time relaxing in the countryside.

A Pope and a Patron

By the time Paul IV died in 1559, Michelangelo was 84 years old and his health was failing. The new pope, Pius IV (Cardinal Giovanni

Michelangelo's Porta Pia was a gate in the Aurelian Walls of Rome that was named after Pope Pius IV.

Angelo de' Medici) was, fortunately, a patron of the arts. He restored part of Michelangelo's pension and gave him complete control over St. Peter's Basilica. Despite failing eyesight and other medical conditions, Michelangelo worked on designs for Rome's Sforza Chapel at the Basilica of Saint Mary Major and a restoration of the Church of Santa Maria degli Angeli. His last architectural project, in 1561, was the renovation of the city gate known as the Porta Pia and the surrounding area of the city, which was completed in 1565, after Michelangelo's death.

As Michelangelo's life came to an end, he was often lonely, sad, and frustrated. Most of his family and friends had died long before him, and although he kept sculpting and drawing, he recognized his passion was running out. Now, his thoughts turned to the subjects he had spent so much of his life trying to capture: Jesus, religion, and personal salvation.

CHAPTER SIX

The Widow and the Muse

As Michelangelo approached the end of his long life, one of his most enduring questions was if he would obtain salvation after he died. The close and loving relationships he had made with people outside of his family played a huge role in that question for him, especially his love for two people: poet Vittoria Colonna and muse Tommaso de' Cavalieri. The artist's deep connection to both of them touched on his devoutness to God and his passion for art.

A Unique Friendship

Although historians are not sure when Michelangelo and the widowed Vittoria Colonna met, they know that the two became very close friends. Soon after losing her husband, Colonna began writing poetry and was a frequent guest in literary circles. When the poet and artist met, it was an instant connection over a shared love of art and religion. Wallace wrote, "Drawings and poems poured forth from the artist. He was the eager admirer; she the appreciative but slightly more restrained recipient of ardent affections. They spent time in each other's company."[67]

Michelangelo wrote many poems for Colonna, including a poem about the widow herself and how he saw her:

This painting by Francesco Vinea, who lived from 1845 to 1902, shows Michelangelo reciting poetry to Vittoria Colonna.

When the prime mover of
many sighs
Heaven took through death from
out her earthly place,
Nature, that never made so fair
a face,
Remained ashamed, and tears
were in all eyes.
O fate, unheeding my
impassioned cries!
O hopes fallacious! O thou spirit
of grace,
Where art thou now? Earth holds
in its embrace
Thy lovely limbs, thy holy
thoughts
the skies.
Vainly did cruel death attempt
to stay

The rumor of thy virtuous
renown,
That Lethe's waters could not
wash away!
A thousand leaves, since he hath
stricken thee down,
Speak of thee, not to thee could
Heaven convey,
Except through death, a refuse
and a crown.[68]

Secret Meetings

Another connection between Colonna and Michelangelo was they were both members of a secret group called the Spirituali. This group met often to debate and discuss religious topics such as divine grace, the logic of the scriptures,

Taking Care of Family

Michelangelo took family responsibility very seriously and supported his brother Buonarroto's two surviving children, Francesca and Lionardo. He provided the dowry (a wedding gift of money) when Francesca married in 1537 and advised Lionardo when it was time to take a wife.

Lionardo and Michelangelo wrote to each other often and grew quite close. The nephew often sent his uncle articles of clothing, wine, and food, and when Michelangelo became ill on several occasions, Lionardo hurried to Rome to be with him. Each time, the artist survived, and he scolded his nephew for only visiting to preserve his inheritance.

When Lionardo married Cassandra di Donato Ridolfi in 1553, Michelangelo gave her expensive jewelry as a wedding gift. Cassandra gave birth to a son in April 1554. They named him Buonarroto. Lionardo and his wife had several more children, including a son they named Michelangelo, though most of the children were born after the aging artist's death. Michelangelo did, however, get to know his grandnephew, who guaranteed a continuation of the family line. Young Buonarroto Buonarroti was 10 when his famous great-uncle died.

and the existence of heaven and hell. English cardinal Reginald Pole was one of the Spiritualis, as well as Cardinal Giovanni Morone, Michelangelo's religious mentor, who was later imprisoned by Pope Paul IV for heresy.

The group explored many controversial religious concepts, including the idea that salvation might truly come from faith, not good works, and that the church should not necessarily be a mediator between God and people. They questioned the absolute authority of the pope and the celibacy of the priests. These unorthodox ideas undermined the power of the church in Rome, and members of the Spirituali group were harassed or persecuted as heretics. The pope, however, was willing to overlook Michelangelo because of his fame and talent. When Cardinal Pole returned to England in 1551, the Spirituali soon disbanded.

A Deep Grief

When Colonna died in 1547, Michelangelo was devastated. The two of them had reached a unique spiritual awareness, and the artist depended on his friend for affection, support, and understanding.

Michelangelo wrote several sonnets in response to her death. They dealt with the aging artist's love and grief and the certainty of death. In "To Vittoria Colonna," Michelangelo proclaimed,

*When she who was the cause of
   all my sighs,*
*Departed from the world, herself,
   and me,*
*Nature, who fain had made us
   worthy her,*
*Rested ashamed, and who had
   seen her wept.*
*But let not boastful Death, who
   quenched the light*
*Of this our sun of suns, be all
   too vain;*
*Since love hath conquered him,
   and let her live,*
*Both here on earth and 'mong
   the saints above.*
*It seemed a cruel and
   unrighteous thing*
*For Death to make her scattered
   virtues dumb,*
*And bear her soul where it might
   show less fair.*
*But (contradiction strange!) her
   writings now*
*Make her more living than she
   was in life;*
*And heaven receives her dead,
   where she had else no part.*[69]

A Handsome Muse

The relationship between the artist and widow was a profound and a platonic one. The relationship between the handsome young Tomasso de' Cavalieri and Michelangelo, however, is unclear. When the two first met, Michelangelo, a known admirer of the male body on canvas, was struck by Cavalieri's physical beauty and seemed instantly infatuated. The two exchanged letters discussing their fondness and respect for each other, and Michelangelo gave Cavalieri

The loss of Vittoria Colonna was monumental to Michelangelo as he felt he had lost one of the few female connections in his life. Shown here is a painting by Francesco Jacovacci of Michelangelo kissing Colonna's hand.

several drawings as gifts. According to Antonio Forcellino,

The three drawings … all depict subjects that allude to the torments

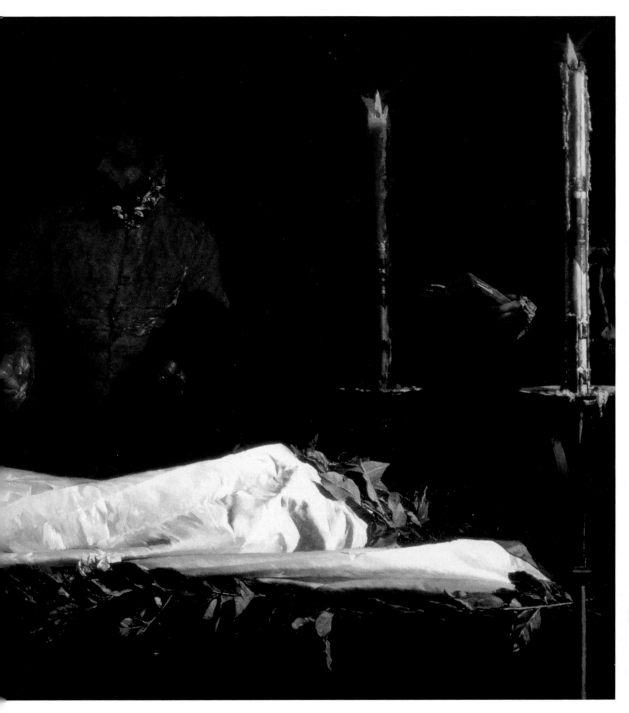

The Widow and the Muse **81**

of love: Phaethon falling from the sky for having dared to come too close to the sun, a metaphor for the presumption of which Michelangelo felt guilty for having approached young Tommaso,

Many art experts have analyzed these drawings in an attempt to figure out what message they had for the young Cavalieri.

himself a "sun"; Tityus tormented by Zeus' eagle for having stolen fire from the gods, and chained to a rock like a lover to his loved one; and the abduction of Ganymede by Zeus' eagle, which

was a metaphor for the soul raised up to the heavens by the sentiment of love.[70]

Luciano Berti wrote in *The Complete Work of Michelangelo* that "In point of fact these drawings are nothing more nor less than equivalents of love poems, in which the eros [love] is manifested and at the same time holds itself back … while betraying a dark background of remorse and conflict."[71]

The letters and sonnets exchanged between the two men should be read in light of 16th-century customs and values, when older men advised younger men as their mentors and mutually exchanged impassioned letters or sonnets of love and friendship that were considered socially acceptable at the time. In a letter from July 1533, Michelangelo wrote to Cavalieri, "I realize now that I could [as soon] forget your name as forget the food on which I live — nay, I could sooner forget the food on which I live, which unhappily nourishes only the body, than your name, which nourishes body and soul, filling both with such delight that I am insensible to sorrow or fear of death, while my memory of you endures."[72]

In a sonnet thought to be dedicated to Cavalieri, Michelangelo wrote,

Through your clear eyes I view a beauteous light,
That my dark sight would ever seek in vain;
With your firm steps a burden I support,
Which my weak power was never used to bear.
I soar aloft, unplumed, upon your wings,
By your intelligence to heaven am raised;
Your smile or frown maketh me pale or red,
Cold in the sun, warm 'mid severest chills.
In your will is mine own will ever fixed;
My thoughts find birth and growth within your heart;
My words are from your spirit only drawn;
And like the moon, alone in heaven, I seem,
That to our eyes were indiscernible,
Save by that light which from the sun proceeds.[73]

Cavalieri remained a good friend to Michelangelo for nearly 30 years and was by his side when the great artist died in Rome in 1564.

The Mystery Surrounding Michelangelo

During Michelangelo's time, homosexuality was strictly outlawed, and punishment was severe. Therefore, the question of Michelangelo's sexuality and how it influenced his art remains unanswered as there is no

Altering Artwork

Shortly after the death of Michelangelo, his assistant and friend Daniele da Volterra was commissioned by Pope Pius IV to paint loincloths, fig leafs, and draperies over most of the nudity in *The Last Judgment* in accordance with the Council of Trent decree. According to the website of the Uffizi Gallery in Florence, Volterra became "infamously known as Il Braghettone, which means the breeches-maker,"[1] although he was a fine artist in his own right.

Volterra covered up half the figures in the fresco but stopped when Pope Pius IV died and the scaffolding had to be removed so a new pope could be elected. The new pope, Pius V, seriously considered destroying all classical antiquities in Rome including the Colosseum and arches throughout the city, as well as the classical statues on private and public display. He regarded the artwork to be pagan, diverting visitors' attention away from St. Peter's Basilica and the other beautiful Roman churches. Fortunately, he ultimately decided against these actions.

1. "Daniele Ricciarelli da Volterra," Virtual Uffizi Gallery, accessed on May 8, 2018. www.virtualuffizi.com/biography/Daniele-Ricciarelli-da-Volterra.htm.

solid proof one way or the other. Condivi wrote that Michelangelo admired and loved the human body and he painted mainly male nudes, so some in the 16th century openly questioned his sexuality. Michelangelo asked, "Whose judgment would be so barbarous as not to appreciate that the foot of a man is more noble than his boot, and his skin more noble than that of a sheep, with which he is dressed?"[74] Beck wrote, "The fact that he admired and rendered marvelous images of young men cannot be used as evidence of latent or real homosexuality, nor, for that matter, can the emasculation of his woman subjects." Beck continued,

"Michelangelo did not use female models and never drew a nude woman from life, basing his renderings on males, usually his studio boys, as was customary."[75]

Forcellino disagreed, believing that Michelangelo was tormented by his repressed sexuality. In his biography *Michelangelo: A Tormented Life*, Forcellino wrote, "There can be no doubt that Michelangelo suffered from his tortured and turbulent personality, his repressed … homosexuality, and his diffidence, which transformed into a persecution complex on encountering the least problem." Forcellino noted that Michelangelo was "in a state of continuous

Historians believe the Rondanini Pietà *was
likely sculpted for Michelangelo's own tomb.*

guilt"[76] because of beliefs about homosexuality during that time.

What historians do know is that Michelangelo publicly admitted he was a platonic lover of men and considered it the highest form of friendship, as did many others in Renaissance Italy. This spiritual, non-physical type of love inspired many of Michelangelo's masterpieces.

"A Form of Prayer"

According to Wallace, Michelangelo focused primarily on carving in his final years of life. "It seems that carving was a form of prayer, a way of bringing himself closer to God. Salvation through creation."[77]

Michelangelo worked on the *Rondanini Pietà* until six days before he died. It was 6 feet 3 inches (1.9 m) high and consisted of just the two standing figures of Christ and Mary, which seemingly merged into one another. Lutz Heusinger wrote about "the unity between Mother and Son" and stated, "It is almost impossible to tell whether it is the Mother supporting the Son, or the Son supporting the Mother, overcome by despair. Both are in need of help, and both hold themselves up in the act of invocation and lament before the world and God."[78]

Michelangelo destroyed his first version, and in the second unfinished pietà, there is an arm in mid-air, wrote Wallace, that "is a ghostly remnant of an earlier composition."[79]

Michelangelo also worked on a series of drawings of the Crucifixion as if, according to Wallace, he was in physical contact with God. His art and poetry centered on the themes of death and sorrow:

Ah, woe is me! Alas! When
*   I revolve*
My years gone by, wearied, I find
*   not one*
Wherein to call a single day
*   my own.*
Fallacious hopes, desires as vain,
*   and thoughts*
Of love compounded and of
*   lover's woes*
(No mortal joy has novelty
*   for me),*
Make up the sum; I know, I feel,
*   't is so.*
Thus have I ever strayed from
*   Truth and Good:*
Where'er I go, shifting from right
*   to left,*
Denser the shades, less bright the
*   sun appears,*
And I, infirm and worn, am nigh
*   to fall.*[80]

A Soul to God

By the end of 1563, the 88-year-old artist was struggling with the weakness and sleepiness the cold, rainy weather brought. When awake, Michelangelo was still sharp and lucid, but his condition deteriorated to the point where a friend reached out to Michelangelo's only heir and nephew, Lionardo, to come to Rome.

After a carving session on the *Rondanini Pietà*, Michelangelo began feeling feverish and sick. He ordered his drawings, sketches, and cartoons burned so that, Giorgio Vasari wrote, "no one should perceive his labours and the efforts of his genius, that he might not appear less than perfect."[81] As the artist got worse, his physician and friends (including Cavalieri) gathered around him. Michelangelo then stated his will out loud, "leaving his soul to God, his body to the earth, and his property to his nearest relations."[82]

Michelangelo died on February 18, 1564, less than 3 weeks before his 89th birthday. A number of religious-centered cartoons were found in his home, but that was it. Beck believes that Michelangelo may have destroyed everything else. "He gathered together his much-guarded drawings and cartoons, over which he had been especially secretive, and set them to flames. Could some have been too pagan or sexually explicit?" Beck asked. "We shall never know."[83] Both the church and Duke Cosimo de' Medici of Florence were extremely disappointed that the famed artist had not left behind any finished paintings or sculptures. The *Rondanini Pietà* and what cartoons remained were seized by church officials. A sealed box that contained 8,000 gold ducats was left for Lionardo.

Return to Florence

Surprisingly, little of value was found when an inventory of Michelangelo's belongings was taken the morning after he died. Forcellino wrote, "A few 'threadbare' items of clothing, 'an iron bedstead with sack of straw, three mattresses, two white woolen blankets and one of white lambskin' … no piece of furniture of any value, no pictures and no precious objects." He added, "But one by one, they pulled out dented copper vases, chipped ceramic ones, knotted handkerchiefs and worn sacks … The notary searched the house … for precious furnishings, mirrors, silverware, gold-plate, damasks and oriental silk. But he found none of this—none of what you would have expected to find in the house of any affluent man in Rome."[84]

The pope wanted Michelangelo to be buried in Rome, but the artist had stated a few days before his death his wish to be buried in Florence. Lionardo, who arrived in Rome three days after his uncle died, secretly and with Cosimo's help, wrapped up Michelangelo's corpse and, according to Vasari, "removed the body from Rome and forwarded it to Florence like merchandise."[85] The cold weather preserved the remains that arrived in Florence on March 11. The Medicis helped to

Many people come to the Basilica di Santa Croce in Firenze, Italy, each year to honor the memory of Michelangelo.

Villa for Sale

In 2018, realtors in Chianti, Italy, gave art lovers with a spare $9.3 million a chance at a one-of-a-kind buy: Michelangelo's Tuscan villa. The 12,916-square-foot (1,200 sq m) residence had been purchased by Michelangelo in 1549. It remained in the Buonarroti family for more than three centuries. The 10-bedroom, 7-bath home had since been restored, and whomever purchased the villa would even be given a copy of the original deed.

Although the artist bought the home in mid-16th century, the actual building is much older. Real estate broker Debbie Fisher stated, "It's exciting to imagine all that has happened on this property since 1047, the year the original tower on the property was built."[1] Inside the home are brick vaulted ceilings, arched doorways, stone fireplaces, terra-cotta floors, and beamed ceilings. It is surrounded by 6 acres (2.4 ha) of land with hundreds of cypress and olive trees.

1. Quoted in Jennifer Baum Lagdameo, "You Can Own Michelangelo's Former Tuscan Villa for $9.3M," *Dwell*, March 26, 2018. www.dwell.com/article/you-can-own-michelangelos-former-tuscan-villa-for-dollar9.3m-7ee32aad.

prepare an elaborate funeral and the creation of a tomb in the Buonarroti family church at Santa Croce. Many thousands came out for the memorial service in his honor.

Michelangelo had finally come home to Florence.

Changing the Role

When young Michelangelo Buonarroti decided to become an artist, it was not a popular choice with his family or in society. An artist was lower class, similar to a workman or craftsman, and certainly beneath the status of a noble family from Florence. His father felt shame and did not hide his disappointment from his teenage son. Little did anyone realize that Michelangelo would be the person who would change the world's view of artists. His talent and passion elevated the role of artist and sculptor in society. His career brought him wealth and status. He was not only famous, but also admired and respected worldwide. He was friends with kings, popes, noblemen, and cardinals. Everyone clamored for a work of art by the great artist.

Despite his wealth and fame, Michelangelo always felt like he was still learning. As he once stated, "If people knew how hard I worked to get my mastery, it wouldn't seem so wonderful at all."[86]

Michelangelo influenced many artists of his time and countless others who followed long after his death. His works still captivate and amaze millions who flock to museums and art galleries. In fact, the "Michelangelo: Divine Draftsman and Designer" exhibition that was held at the Metropolitan Museum of Art in New York City from November 2017 through February 2018 became the museum's 10th most visited exhibition of all time. More than 700,000 people viewed Michelangelo's works at the Met during the 3 months they were on display. It is likely that people will want to experience firsthand the imagination, spirit, and insight of Michelangelo and his enduring masterpieces for many years to come.

Notes

Introduction: An Artistic Genius

1. Giorgio Vasari, *The Lives of the Painters, Sculptors, and Architects, Volume Eight*. Trans. A. B. Hinds. London, UK: J. M. Dent & Company, 1800, p. 155.
2. Jayne Pettit, *Michelangelo: Genius of the Renaissance*. New York, NY: Franklin Watts, 1998, p. 11.
3. William E. Wallace, *Michelangelo: The Artist, the Man, and His Times*. New York, NY: Cambridge University Press, 2010, p. 340.
4. Vasari, *Lives of the Painters, Sculptors, and Architects*, p. 3.
5. Vasari, *Lives of the Painters, Sculptors, and Architects*, p. 105.
6. Antonio Forcellino, *Michelangelo: A Tormented Life*. Cambridge, UK: Polity, 2010, pp. 5, 10.
7. Quoted in Vasari, *Lives of the Painters, Sculptors, and Architects*, p. 110.

Chapter One: A Family, a Struggle, and a Choice

8. Quoted in Thomas Cahill, *Heretics and Heroes: How Renaissance Artists and Reformation Priests Created Our World*. New York, NY: Anchor Books, 2013, p. 109.
9. George Bull, *Michelangelo: A Biography*. New York, NY: St. Martin's, 1996, p. 9.
10. Wallace, *Michelangelo*, p. 32.
11. Ascanio Condivi, "The Life of Michael Angelo Buonarroti" in *Michael Angelo Buonarroti*. Trans. Charles

Holroyd. London, UK: Duckworth and Co., 1903, p. 7.

12. Forcellino, *Michelangelo*, p. 21.

13. Bull, *Michelangelo*, p. 21.

14. Condivi, "Life of Michael Angelo Buonarroti," p. 13.

15. Condivi, "Life of Michael Angelo Buonarroti," p. 81.

Chapter Two: Trying His Luck Elsewhere

16. Condivi, "Life of Michael Angelo Buonarroti," p. 24.

17. Giorgio Vasari, *The Life of Michelangelo*. Trans. A. B. Hinds. Los Angeles, CA: J. Paul Getty Museum, 2018, p. 52.

18. Quoted in John T. Spike, *Young Michelangelo: The Path to the Sistine*. New York, NY: Vendome Press, 2010, pp. 109–110.

19. Condivi, "Life of Michael Angelo Buonarroti," p. 25.

20. Joachim Poeschke, *Michelangelo and His World: Sculpture of the Italian Renaissance*. New York, NY: Harry N. Abrams, 1996, p. 75.

21. Wallace, *Michelangelo*, p. 23.

22. Spike, *Young Michelangelo*, p. 126.

23. Umberto Baldini, "Sculpture" in *The Complete Work of Michelangelo*. Novara, Italy: Barnes & Noble by arrangement with Orbis, 1996, p. 104.

24. Poeschke, *Michelangelo and His World*, p. 86.

25. Condivi, "Life of Michael Angelo Buonarroti," p. 28.

26. Vasari, *Life of Michelangelo*, p. 59.

27. Forcellino, *Michelangelo*, p. 64.

28. James Beck, *Three Worlds of Michelangelo*. New York, NY: W. W. Norton, 1999, p. 142.

Chapter Three: The Artist and the Pope

29. Lutz Heusinger, *Michelangelo: Life and Works in Chronological Order*. New York, NY: Harper & Row, 1982, p. 16.

30. Quoted in Condivi, "Life of Michael Angelo Buonarroti," p. 35.

31. Ross King, *Michelangelo & the Pope's Ceiling*. New York,

NY: Walker & Co., 2003, pp. 53–54.

32. King, *Michelangelo & the Pope's Ceiling*, p. 245.

33. King, *Michelangelo & the Pope's Ceiling*, p. 266.

34. Bull, *Michelangelo*, p. 99.

35. Quoted in Michelangelo Buonarroti, *Selected Poems from Michelangelo Buonarroti*. Ed. Ednah D. Cheney. New York, NY: Lee and Shepard, 1885, p. 61.

36. Quoted in Condivi, "Life of Michael Angelo Buonarroti," p. 45.

37. Vasari, *Life of Michelangelo*, pp. 94, 96.

38. Quoted in Bull, *Michelangelo*, p. 104.

39. Quoted in King, *Michelangelo & the Pope's Ceiling*, p. 291.

40. Quoted in Wallace, *Michelangelo*, p. 105.

41. Forcellino, *Michelangelo*, p. 110.

42. Baldini, "Sculpture," p. 115.

Chapter Four: The Medicis and Michelangelo

43. Lauren Mitchell Ruehring, "Michelangelo Biography," HowStuffWorks, August 20, 2007. entertainment. howstuffworks.com/arts/ artwork/michelangelo- biography4.htm.

44. Bull, *Michelangelo*, p. 133.

45. Bull, *Michelangelo*, p. 137.

46. Quoted in Bull, *Michelangelo*, pp. 140–141.

47. Wallace, *Michelangelo*, p. 121.

48. Quoted in Wallace, *Michelangelo*, p. 145.

49. Wallace, *Michelangelo*, pp. 149–150.

50. Wallace, *Michelangelo*, p. 151.

51. Wallace, *Michelangelo*, p. 152.

52. Wallace, *Michelangelo*, p. 154.

53. Bull, *Michelangelo*, p. 215.

54. Quoted in Buonarroti, *Selected Poems*, p. 139.

55. Quoted in "Michelangelo Drawings of His Muse Go on Display," BBC News, February 18, 2010. news.bbc. co.uk/2/hi/entertainment/ arts_and_culture/8520879. stm.

Chapter Five: At His Peak

56. Forcellino, *Michelangelo*, p. 193.

57. Wallace, *Michelangelo*, p. 185.

58. Vasari, *Lives of the Painters, Sculptors, and Architects*, p. 55.
59. Forcellino, *Michelangelo*, pp. 194–195.
60. Wallace, *Michelangelo*, pp. 251–252.
61. Bull, *Michelangelo*, p. 329.
62. Quoted in Jack Adler, "Michelangelo" in *Splendid Seniors: Great Lives, Great Deeds*. Nashville, TN: Pearlsong Press, 2007.
63. Wallace, *Michelangelo*, p. 224.
64. Forcellino, *Michelangelo*, p. 275.
65. Wallace, *Michelangelo*, p. 228.
66. Baldini, "Sculpture," p. 350.

Chapter Six: The Widow and the Muse

67. Wallace, *Michelangelo*, p. 213.
68. Michelangelo Buonarroti, "To Vittoria Colonna," Poetry Archive, accessed on May 3, 2018. www.poetry-archive. com/b/to_vittoria_colonna. html.
69. Buonarroti, *Selected Poems*, p. 115.
70. Forcellino, *Michelangelo*, pp. 187–188.
71. Luciano Berti, "Drawings," in *The Complete Work of Michelangelo*. Novara, Italy: Barnes & Noble by arrangement with Orbis, 1996, p. 452.
72. Quoted in Christopher Ryan, *The Poetry of Michelangelo: An Introduction*. Madison, NJ: Fairleigh Dickinson University Press, 1998, p. 94.
73. Quoted in Buonarroti, *Selected Poems*, p. 85.
74. Quoted in Beck, *Three Worlds of Michelangelo*, pp. 151–152.
75. Beck, *Three Worlds of Michelangelo*, p. 152.
76. Forcellino, *Michelangelo*, p. 206.
77. Wallace, *Michelangelo*, p. 321.
78. Heusinger, *Michelangelo*, pp. 31–32.
79. Wallace, *Michelangelo*, p. 321.
80. Quoted in Buonarroti, *Selected Poems*, p. 135.
81. Vasari, *Lives of the Painters, Sculptors, and Architects*, pp. 100–101.
82. Vasari, *Lives of the Painters, Sculptors, and Architects*, p. 99.
83. Beck, *Three Worlds of Michelangelo*, p. 231.
84. Forcellino, *Michelangelo*, p. 294.

85. Vasari, *Lives of the Painters, Sculptors, and Architects,* p. 118.

86. Quoted in "Michelangelo Quotes," Michelangelo Gallery, accessed on May 11, 2018. www.michelangelo-gallery.com/quotes.aspx.

For More Information

Books

Avery, Victoria. *Michelangelo: Sculptor in Bronze*. London, UK: Philip Wilson Publishers Ltd., 2018.
> This book examines two bronze statues that were attributed to Michelangelo in 2015.

Richardson, Adele. *Michelangelo*. Mankato, MN: Creative Education, 2017.
> Richardson's biography of Michelangelo explores the artist's life, works, and relationships.

Vasari, Giorgio. *The Life of Michelangelo*. Los Angeles, CA: J. Paul Getty Museum, 2018.
> Vasari's classic biography of Michelangelo was originally published in the mid-16th century. Today, the book features a new introduction and 42 images of the artist's works.

Zöllner, Frank, and Christof Thoenes. *Michelangelo: The Complete Paintings, Sculptures, and Architecture*. Köln, Germany: Taschen, 2017.
> This book features a collection of Michelangelo's numerous works and also includes a biographical essay.

Websites

Michelangelo
www.history.com/topics/michelangelo
> This page on the History Channel website features interesting facts about the artist as well as videos.

"Michelangelo's Secret Message in the Sistine Chapel: A Juxtaposition of God and the Human Brain"
blogs.scientificamerican.com/guest-blog/michelangelos-secret-message-in-the-sistine-chapel-a-juxtaposition-of-god-and-the-human-brain/
> This guest blog on the *Scientific American* website explores the idea that Michelangelo may have left secret messages in his works.

Vatican Museums: Ceiling
mv.vatican.va/3_EN/pages/CSN/CSN_Volta.html
> This Vatican Museum website provides details about Michelangelo's Sistine Chapel ceiling.

"What Is the Greatest Michelangelo? The 10 Most Iconic Works by the Renaissance Titan, Ranked"
news.artnet.com/opinion/michelangelos-10-most-popular-works-ranked-1144943
> The ArtNet News website shares what it believes are Michelangelo's 10 most iconic works and provides more information about each piece.

Index

Picture Credits

Cover (screen image) Rawpixel.com/Shutterstock.com; cover (main image), p. 77 DEA/G. NIMATALLAH/De Agostini Picture Library/Getty Images; pp. 1, 3, 4, 6, 10, 22, 36, 52, 62, 76, 92, 97, 99, 103, 104 (big paint swatch) Lunarus/Shutterstock.com; p. 8 DEA PICTURE LIBRARY/De Agostini Picture Library/Getty Images; p. 11 Gjon Mili/The LIFE Picture Collection/Getty Images; p. 12 DEA/A. DAGLI ORTI/De Agostini Picture Library/Getty Images; p. 13 (main) Courtesy of the Library of Congress; pp. 13, 30, 42, 46, 65 (paint caption background) Jaroslav Machacek/Shutterstock.com; p. 15 British Museum, London, UK/Bridgeman Images; p. 18 Thekla Clark/Corbis via Getty Images; p. 20 Courtesy of the Metropolitan Museum of Art, New York; p. 23 Bruno Balestrini/Electa/Mondadori Portfolio via Getty Images; pp. 26–27 Vitaly Minko/Shutterstock.com; p. 29 jorisvo/Shutterstock.com; pp. 30, 32 Franco Origlia/Getty Images; p. 33 Alinari Archives/Corbis/Corbis via Getty Images; pp. 38–39 Alessandro Colle/Shutterstock.com; pp. 40–41 Michelangelo Buonarroti/Getty Images; pp. 42–43 PHAS/UIG via Getty Images; pp. 46–47 RPBaiao/Shutterstock.com; p. 50 Danilo Ascione/Shutterstock.com; p. 53 Leemage/Corbis via Getty Images; pp. 56–57, 59, 80–81, 86 DeAgostini/Getty Images; pp. 63, 64–65 Mondadori Portfolio via Getty Images; p. 67 Leemage/UIG via Getty Images; p. 68 RODKARV/Shutterstock.com; pp. 70–71 4thebirds/Shutterstock.com; p. 71 (inset) Alfredo Cerra/Shutterstock.com; p. 74 Fine Art Images/Heritage Images/Getty Images; pp. 82–83 BEN STANSALL/AFP/Getty Images; p. 89 Robert Alexander/Getty Images; back cover vector illustration/Shutterstock.com.

About the Author

Tamra B. Orr is the author of more than 500 nonfiction books for readers of all ages. She lives in the Pacific Northwest with her family and spends her free time writing letters to people all over the world and tent camping throughout the state. Orr graduated from Ball State University with a degree in secondary education but found she would rather write about the world than anything else. She struggles to draw a legible stick figure and hopes that by writing about Michelangelo, a little of his talent will soak in.